CUSTOM CURRI

Streetwise

Fran and Jill Sciacca

Rick Thompson

David C. Cook Publishing Co.
Elgin, Illinois—Weston, Ontario

Custom Curriculum
Streetwise

© 1994 David C. Cook Publishing Co.

All rights reserved. Except for the reproducible student sheets, which may be copied for ministry use, no part of this book may be reproduced in any form without the written permission of the publisher, unless otherwise noted in the text.

Unless otherwise noted, Scripture quotations are from the Holy Bible, New International Version (NIV), © 1973, 1978, 1984 by International Bible Society. Used by permission of Zondervan Bible Publishers.

Published by David C. Cook Publishing Co.
850 North Grove Ave., Elgin, IL 60120
Cable address: DCCOOK
Series creator: John Duckworth
Series editor: Randy Southern
Editor: Randy Southern
Option writers: John Duckworth, Nelson E. Copeland, Jr., Michelle Geiman, and Lisa Anderson
Designer: Bill Paetzold
Cover illustrator: Eric Masi
Inside illustrator: Eric Masi
Printed in U.S.A.

ISBN: 0-7814-5150-7

CONTENTS

About the Authors — 4

You've Made the Right Choice! — 5

Getting the Most out of Proverbs and Ecclesiastes
by Fran and Jill Sciacca — 9

Publicity Clip Art — 12

Sessions by Rick Thompson
Options by John Duckworth, Nelson E. Copeland, Jr., Michelle Geiman, and Lisa Anderson

Session One
Words of Wisdom
14

Session Two
A Fool and His Happiness Are Soon Parted
30

Session Three
Hold Your Tongue!
46

Session Four
The Meaning of Life
64

Session Five
A Matter of Time
80

About the Authors

Rick Thompson is managing editor of youth and young adult products at David C. Cook. Active in youth work at his church, Rick wrote *Unseen Mysteries* for the Custom Curriculum series. He is also a contributor to the Hot Topics Youth Electives series (Cook).

John Duckworth is a writer and illustrator in Carol Stream, Illinois. He has worked with teenagers in youth groups and Sunday school, written several books including *The School Zone* (SonPower) and *Face to Face with Jesus* (in the Custom Curriculum series), and created such youth resources as Hot Topics Youth Electives and Snap Sessions for David C. Cook.

Nelson E. Copeland, Jr., is a nationally known speaker and the author of several youth resources including *Great Games for City Kids* (Youth Specialties) and *A New Agenda for Urban Youth* (Winston-Derek). He is president of the Christian Education Coalition for African-American Leadership (CECAAL), an organization dedicated to reinforcing educational and cultural excellence among urban teenagers. He also serves as youth pastor at the First Baptist Church in Morton, Pennsylvania.

Michelle Geiman is a free-lance writer living in Carol Stream, Illinois.

Lisa Anderson is a free-lance writer living in Wolverton, Minnesota.

You've Made the Right Choice!

Thanks for choosing **Custom Curriculum!** We think your choice says at least three things about you:

(1) You know your group pretty well, and want your program to fit that group like a glove;

(2) You like having options instead of being boxed in by some far-off curriculum editor;

(3) You have a small mole on your left forearm, exactly two inches below the elbow.

OK, so we were wrong about the mole. But if you like having choices that help you tailor meetings to fit your kids, **Custom Curriculum** *is* the best place to be.

Going through Customs

In this (and every) **Custom Curriculum** volume, you'll find
- five great sessions you can use anytime, in any order.
- reproducible student handouts, at least one per session.
- a truckload of options for adapting the sessions to your group (more about that in a minute).
- a helpful get-you-ready article by a youth expert.
- clip art for making posters, fliers, and other kinds of publicity to get kids to your meetings.

Each **Custom Curriculum** session has three to six steps. No matter how many steps a session has, it's designed to achieve these goals:

• *Getting together.* Using an icebreaker activity, you'll help kids be glad they came to the meeting.

• *Getting thirsty.* Why should kids care about your topic? Why should they care what the Bible has to say about it? You'll want to take a few minutes to earn their interest before you start pouring the "living water."

• *Getting the Word.* By exploring and discussing carefully selected passages, you'll find out what God has to say.

• *Getting the point.* Here's where you'll help kids make the leap from principles to nitty-gritty situations they are likely to face.

• *Getting personal.* What should each group member do as a result of this session? You'll help each person find a specific "next step" response that works for him or her.

Each session is written to last 45 to 60 minutes. But what if you have less time—or more? No problem! **Custom Curriculum** is all about . . . options!

What Are My Options?

Every **Custom Curriculum** session gives you fourteen kinds of options:

• *Extra Action*—for groups that learn better when they're physically moving (instead of just reading, writing, and discussing).

• *Combined Junior High/High School*—to use when you're mixing age levels, and an activity or case study would be too "young" or "old" for part of the group.

• *Small Group*—for adapting activities that would be tough with groups of fewer than eight kids.

• *Large Group*—to alter steps for groups of more than twenty kids.

• *Urban*—for fitting sessions to urban facilities and multiethnic (especially African-American) concerns.

• *Heard It All Before*—for fresh approaches that get past the defenses of kids who are jaded by years in church.

• *Little Bible Background*—to use when most of your kids are strangers to the Bible, or haven't made a Christian commitment.

• *Mostly Guys*—to focus on guys' interests and to substitute activities they might be more enthused about.

• *Mostly Girls*—to address girls' concerns and to substitute activities they might prefer.

• *Extra Fun*—for longer, more "rowdy" youth meetings where the emphasis is on fun.

• *Short Meeting Time*—tips for condensing the session to 30 minutes or so.

• *Fellowship & Worship*—for building deeper relationships or enabling kids to praise God together.

• *Media*—to spice up meetings with video, music, or other popular media.

• *Sixth Grade*—appearing only in junior high/middle school volumes, this option helps you change steps that sixth graders might find hard to understand or relate to.

• *Extra Challenge*—appearing only in high school volumes, this option lets you crank up the voltage for kids who are ready for more Scripture or more demanding personal application.

Each kind of option is offered twice in each session. So in this book, you get *almost 150* ways to tweak the meetings to fit your group!

Customizing a Session

All right, you may be thinking. *With all of these options flying around, how do I put a session together? I don't have a lot of time, you know.*

We know! That's why we've made **Custom Curriculum** as easy to follow as possible. Let's take a look at how you might prepare an actual meeting. You can do that in four easy steps:

(1) *Read the basic session plan.* Start by choosing one or more of the goals listed at the beginning of the session. You have three to pick from: a goal that emphasizes *knowledge,* one that stresses *understanding,* and one that emphasizes *action.* Choose one or more, depending on what *you* want to accomplish. Then read the basic plan to see what will work for you and what might not.

(2) *Choose your options.* You don't *have* to use any options at all; the basic session plan would work well for many groups, and you may want

to stick with it if you have absolutely no time to consider options. But if you want a more perfect fit, check out your choices.

As you read the basic session plan, you'll see small symbols in the margin. Each symbol stands for a different kind of option. When you see a symbol, it means that kind of option is offered for that step. Turn to the options section (which can be found immediately following the Repro Resources for each session), look for the category indicated by the symbol, and you'll see that option explained.

Let's say you have a small group, mostly guys who get bored if they don't keep moving. You'll want to keep an eye out for three kinds of options: Small Group, Mostly Guys, and Extra Action. As you read the basic session, you might spot symbols that tell you there are Small Group options for Step 1 and Step 3—maybe a different way to play a game so that you don't need big teams, and a way to cover several Bible passages when just a few kids are looking them up. Then you see symbols telling you that there are Mostly Guys options for Step 2 and Step 4—perhaps a substitute activity that doesn't require too much self-disclosure, and a case study guys will relate to. Finally you see symbols indicating Extra Action options for Step 2 and Step 3—maybe an active way to get kids' opinions instead of handing out a survey, and a way to act out some verses instead of just looking them up.

After reading the options, you might decide to use four of them. You base your choices on your personal tastes and the traits of your group that you think are most important right now. **Custom Curriculum** offers you more options than you'll need, so you can pick your current favorites and plug others into future meetings if you like.

(3) *Use the checklist.* Once you've picked your options, keep track of them with the simple checklist that appears at the end of each option section (just before the start of the next session plan). This little form gives you a place to write down the materials you'll need too—since they depend on the options you've chosen.

(4) *Get your stuff together.* Gather your materials; photocopy any Repro Resources (reproducible student sheets) you've decided to use. And . . . you're ready!

The Custom Curriculum Challenge

Your kids are fortunate to have you as their leader. You see them not as a bunch of generic teenagers, but as real, live, unique kids. You care whether you really connect with them. That's why you're willing to take a few extra minutes to tailor your meetings to fit.

It's a challenge to work with real, live kids, isn't it? We think you deserve a standing ovation for taking that challenge. And we pray that **Custom Curriculum** helps you shape sessions that shape lives for Jesus Christ and His kingdom.

—*The Editors*

Getting the Most out of Proverbs and Ecclesiastes
by Fran and Jill Sciacca

The perfect paradigm of our present American culture is the corner convenience store. These shops thrive on our willingness to pay higher costs for goods and services in exchange for lower levels of inconvenience. Instead of encouraging prudent planning, selection, and control of our appetites, convenience stores stimulate impulse buying and careless spending. And we don't *think* about our wasteful decisions. As a culture, we also are increasingly willing to live with disposable relationships. Many partners choose to exchange long-term responsibility for immediate pleasure. One tragic result of this malady is that the children of the nineties, even churched kids, are growing up with no understanding—much less appreciation—of how to live for the "long haul." Life is viewed more as a quick sprint rather than a marathon, an event more than a process. Paul's parting statement, "I have fought the good fight, I have finished the race, I have kept the faith" (II Timothy 4:7), is a foreign concept and a crazy mentality to many of today's teens.

In *Streetwise* you'll have the opportunity to make significant advances in a very needed area. These sessions plunge headlong into Proverbs and Ecclesiastes, two books of the Bible that help us understand and deal with "convenience store" living, the notion that everything in life should come quickly. King Solomon, often called the wisest man who ever lived, played a role in writing both of these books. Even though God entrusted deep spiritual wisdom to Solomon, He also allowed the king to learn from the crushing consequences brought on by his own sin. Solomon, in short, was very qualified to speak and teach about both wisdom and foolishness.

Proverbs: If It's Important, It's Probably in Here!

The material in Proverbs is profound yet practical. Solomon paints a panoramic portrait of every human relationship we encounter (good *and* bad) with bold yet specific strokes. The first nine chapters address broad subjects using colorful, symbolic language.

Beginning with chapter ten, Proverbs virtually explodes with themes that are the brightest threads in any teen's personal tapestry. Solomon teaches about the differences between a wise man and a fool, and he warns the readers to choose carefully between the two. The tongue is a familiar topic in Proverbs. We are taught about its power to either build up or tear down our reputation and our relationships. Proverbs contains a special focus on the family, including topics like getting along with siblings, the relationship between parents and children, how husbands and wives should treat each other, and even growing old. Friends and friendship also get a lot of press in Proverbs, along with topics like emotions, decision making, true humility, money, and pride.

But Proverbs is more than a careful collection of pithy paradigms or marvelous metaphors about life on planet earth. One of the clearest notions running through the book is shouted in the introduction and echoes until the end: "The *fear of the Lord* is the beginning of knowledge" (1:7, emphasis mine). Help your kids recognize that Proverbs describes life *as it really should be lived,* because it was authored by the Lord of life itself. These are not "Solomon's Suggestions," an early version of Ann Landers! Eliminating God and then trying to figure out how to live a meaningful life is about as easy as pushing a chain. Proverbs begins and ends with the penetrating truth that God must be included in any equation that attempts to explain life and/or how to live it. Truth about living in the *real* world, not trendy suggestions for a "successful" life, is what Proverbs is all about. Its message is timeless because its author is the One who made both the players and the rules.

Ecclesiastes: Bad Choices and Meaninglessness

Ecclesiastes, like parts of Proverbs, probably was written by King Solomon. The primary difference between Ecclesiastes and Proverbs, however, is that Solomon probably wrote Ecclesiastes much later in life. In fact, some think that Ecclesiastes is a sort of "journal" about Solomon's pursuit of meaning in life without God—a search that he says is about as valuable as chasing after the wind! It's the diary of a man who made a career out of making bad choices.

Many people shy away from reading Ecclesiastes because they find it too depressing. After all, any book whose opening statement is "Meaningless! Meaningless!" is not destined for the *New York Times* Bestseller List! However, many readers of Ecclesiastes fail to unlock the beauty of this book because they do not understand the significance of one small phrase that appears and reappears. That phrase is "under the sun." It shows up at least twice in every chapter. "Under the sun" refers to a perspective about life on this planet that does not allow for God. Once you understand that Solomon is penning the memoirs of his own journey to find meaning "under the sun" (without God), the book begins to take on life. It becomes the clearest testimony in Scripture of the futility of living *as if there is no God.* Make sure your kids discover this key early on as you study Ecclesiastes. Ask them if they want to read the diary of someone who had access to every possible toy, tried every possible pleasure and every conceivable token of wealth and success. Most young people would be eager to savor such an opportunity.

Of Ballpoints and Backbones

Solomon indeed "did it all" and "had it all." He filled his mind with knowledge, his stomach with food and wine, his eyes with pleasure, his bedrooms with women, his stalls with horses, his calendar with travel, his vaults with riches, his time with thinking, and his nation with beautiful buildings. But each time he sat down and assessed his accomplishments and fulfillment, the answer was the same: "Meaningless, utterly meaningless!" Why? How do you explain the predictable outcome of his adventures? The answer can be found in a simple statement that summarizes a powerful principle: *Purpose is contingent upon design.*

Each year when we discuss the basis of meaning and purpose in my high school Bible classes, I introduce this notion. It is genuinely exciting to see the lights "come on" in the minds of students. The principle, simply stated, is that the purpose of anything (what it is intended to do and be) is totally dependent upon its design. In other words, the purpose of a ballpoint pen is to write on a limited variety of surfaces, normally paper. It is *not* intended to be used to pry open file cabinets, punch holes in sheetrock, or prop open windows. What's the point? The point is that something finds its purpose in doing what it was designed to do. The opposite is also true. Screwdrivers often break when used as chisels; plastic knives snap when used to exert great force; etc. Now if humans are really the product of random evolution, we are a product of chance, not design. Therefore, we have no purpose. In fact, in an evolutionary scheme, a ballpoint pen has more purpose than a person does because *it* has design and the person doesn't!

However, if humans *were* made in the image of God with a capacity to know Him intimately (Jeremiah 9:23, 24), then trying to live as though that were not true is about as feasible as a fish enjoying a stroll down your street! When a human being seeks to find a purpose in life without God, he or she will eventually be forced to conclude, "Everything is meaningless." As you explore Ecclesiastes, emphasize the fact that Solomon was a man who fought to deny his design, and ended up with no lasting purpose. It wasn't because he failed to discover the right things. Happiness and purpose were not "just around the bend" for Solomon. He had no lasting purpose because he tried to be what he could not—someone who was *not* made in God's image.

Streetwise is designed to do just what the title suggests: make your group members wise about life in the streets at home, school, work, and play. Someone has aptly said that adolescence is like a minefield. Our job is to teach kids how to make it to the other side without becoming another casualty. Two of the best books in the Bible for helping us with this task are Proverbs and Ecclesiastes.

As you prepare to lead these studies, open your own heart and mind to let God speak to you. Let your group members see your life growing to be more in tune with God's design for you, which is intimate fellowship with Him. Young people are yearning for "heroes" who have convictions about what really matters. *Your life* can be a lesson in itself.

Fran and Jill Sciacca have been involved in youth ministry for nearly two decades. Fran is a graduate of Denver Seminary. He has been teaching Christian high school Bible since 1980. Jill has a degree in journalism and sociology and is a full-time homemaker and free-lance writer/editor. She has written for Discipleship Journal *and* Decision *magazine, and has served on the editorial team for the* Youth Bible (Word, Inc.). *Fran and Jill coauthored* Lifelines (Zondervan), *an award-winning Bible study series for high schoolers. Fran is the author of the best-selling Bible study,* To Walk and Not Grow Weary (NavPress), *as well as* Generation at Risk (Moody), *and* Wounded Saints (Baker). *Fran and Jill have four children—two daughters and two sons. The Sciaccas live in Alabaster, Alabama.*

Publicity Clip Art

The images on these two pages are designed to help you promote this course within your church and community. Feel free to photocopy anything here and adapt it to fit your publicity needs. The stuff on this page could be used as a flier that you send or hand out to kids—or as a bulletin insert. The stuff on the next page could be used to add visual interest to newsletters, calendars, bulletin boards, or other promotions. Be creative and have fun!

Don't Be a Fool

What's the difference between being wise and being a fool? Find out as we begin a new course called *Streetwise*. In Proverbs and Ecclesiastes, we'll explore some of the wisest passages ever written. You'll discover practical advice on how to find wisdom, when to take advice, and where to look for true happiness. It would be foolish to miss this opportunity.

Who:

When:

Where:

Questions? Call:

Streetwise

Streetwise

Got something to say?
We'd love to hear it.

Look before you leap.

Things aren't always
as they seem.

SESSION 1

Words of Wisdom

YOUR GOALS FOR THIS SESSION:
Choose one or more

☐ To help kids recognize that wisdom is more than "book knowledge."

☐ To help kids understand that the way to become wise is to get to know God better and follow His ways.

☐ To help kids identify one thing they can do this week to overcome a barrier that keeps them from knowing God better.

☐ Other _____

Your Bible Base:

Proverbs 1:1-7
Various Proverbs that deal with wisdom and the fear of the Lord

CUSTOM CURRICULUM

Who's the Wisest of Them All?

(Needed: Copies of Repro Resource 1, pencils, small prize [optional])

To get kids thinking about what wisdom is and isn't, hand out copies of "Wisdom Test" (Repro Resource 1) and pencils. These Repro Resources could be given to individuals or to teams. As you're handing out the sheets, explain to your group members that this is a test to see how wise they are in certain areas that they probably won't be tested on at school. Give kids a few minutes to work, then go over the answers together.

You might want to mention that the correct answers are like a very naughty taxi—A BAD, BAD CAB (1—A, 2—B, 3—A, 4—D, 5—B, 6—A, 7—D, 8—C, 9—A, 10—B). If you wish, award a small prize to your winner(s)—perhaps a packet of Kleenex (brain tissue).

Then ask: **How accurately do you think this test reflects how wise you really are?** (Not very, because it only covers a few areas—and some of the areas aren't that important. [although #1 could be important if your kids are into eating flowers].)

What would be a better test to measure how wise someone is? Kids might mention things like SAT or ACT tests, essay tests, or other tests. Some might say that it's difficult to measure wisdom through a test. If they do, ask them *why* it's difficult.

Who's the wisest person you know? What makes this person so wise? Let kids share for a few minutes before moving on. Try to get beyond the "correct, churchy" answers like Jesus or Solomon.

What Is Wisdom?

(Needed: Paper, pencils, chalkboard and chalk or newsprint and marker)

Say: **For the next few weeks we'll be taking a look at some parts of the Bible known as the "wisdom literature." We'll** be looking mostly at Proverbs and Ecclesiastes. I guess the logical place to begin, then, is to define "wisdom." **How would you define "wisdom"?** Have kids write their definitions on the back of Repro Resource 1, on the board, or on sheets of newsprint. Encourage them to come up with short definitions, like "being smart," "knowing a lot and how to use it," etc.

After several volunteers have shared their responses, say: **The dictionary defines wisdom as "accumulated philosophic or scientific learning: knowledge; ability to discern inner qualities and relationships: insight; good sense: judgment."** You might want to write these definitions on the board, or at least the three key words: knowledge, insight, and judgment.

Suggest: **A definition that takes the Bible's meaning of the word into account might be "Gaining insight from a study of God's ways and applying what you learn in daily life."**

Ask: **What do you think of these definitions? How is the Bible's definition different from the dictionary's?** (The Bible's definition goes beyond mere head knowledge and refers to how we live our daily lives. The Bible recognizes that God is the true source of all wisdom.)

Why should you care about what wisdom is, anyway? What benefits are there to being wise? Group members may have difficulty answering these questions, but it's essential that you get kids thinking about them. If they don't see any reason or personal benefit from studying about wisdom, they probably won't really care about anything else that follows. Try listing some of the benefits of wisdom. Here are a few ideas to get you started: It helps us avoid mistakes; it helps us make better choices; it helps us get to know God better. (Further benefits are listed in Proverbs 2 and 3. You'll get to those later.)

What might it cost you to become wiser? If you listed some of the benefits, you might also want to list some of the costs. For instance, becoming wiser might mean some changes in lifestyle. Once you gain wisdom in certain areas, you'll be challenged to act on what you've learned. Friends might think you're weird for pursuing wisdom. Becoming wise takes time and effort. (Besides, many people think that ignorance is bliss!)

Summarize: **The bottom line seems to be that there's a real value in seeking after wisdom—but it will cost you something too. Your job as we continue in this study is to decide if the benefits of wisdom outweigh the costs. Only you can make that call.**

CUSTOM CURRICULUM

STEP 3

A Proverbs Primer

(Needed: Bibles, copies of Repro Resource 2, pencils)

OPTIONS: EXTRA ACTION, SMALL GROUP, LARGE GROUP, HEARD IT ALL BEFORE, LITTLE BIBLE BACKGROUND, SHORT MEETING TIME

Ask some questions to see how familiar your kids are with the Book of Proverbs. Can they recite any verses? Do they know who wrote it? Have they ever read it through from start to finish? What are their impressions of the book? Point out that a lot of people have trouble with the book because it seems like a hodge-podge of unrelated verses. Explain that in this session you'll try to sort some of it out.

Read Proverbs 1:1-7 together. Point out that these verses present the purpose and main theme of the book.

Ask: **Why was the book written?** (To help us gain wisdom, discipline, understanding, etc.)

Who was it written for? (The simple, the young [v. 4], wise people who want to add to their learning [v. 5].) Point out that you'll talk more about what it means to be "simple" in the next session.

Hand out copies of "A Proverbs Primer" (Repro Resource 2). Explain: **This sheet contains a few key words from the first seven verses of Proverbs. By understanding these key words, you'll have a better grasp of the whole book.**

Go over the first key word (Proverb) as a group. Point out that what we typically think of as the short-saying type of proverbs don't begin until chapter 10. The first nine chapters serve as an introduction to these sayings. It's as if the first nine chapters are there to show us why we should care about the sayings that follow.

Have group members form teams. Assign each team one or more of the three remaining words or phrases from the sheet. Give the teams a few minutes to look up their assigned passages and answer the questions for their word or phrase. After a few minutes, have the teams report back to the rest of the group what they learned about their word or phrase. Use the following information to supplement your discussion.

Solomon
• *Who was Solomon?* (He was the son of David and Bathsheba. He was a very wise and rich king. He was known for uttering three thousand proverbs during his lifetime [I Kings 4:32]. His many foreign wives and concubines eventually led him away from God.) Point out that when we consider Solomon's downward slide, we need to take a "do as I say, not as I do" approach to the Book of Proverbs.

• *Who wrote the Book of Proverbs?* (Proverbs 1:1 attributes the entire book to Solomon, but other authors are mentioned in different places in the text. The bulk of the book [10:1–22:16; 25:1–29:27] is attributed directly to Solomon. It's possible that he compiled the book, sort of like an editor, or that most of it was compiled during his reign. Proverbs 25–31 were probably added to Solomon's collection at a later date during the reign of King Hezekiah of Judah. The other named authors, Agur and King Lemuel, were most likely Ishmaelites [Arabs]. Solomon was probably quite familiar with the wisdom of neighboring lands.)

Wisdom

• *What other words are used in the book that seem to mean something similar to wisdom?* (Discipline, understanding, insight, prudence, knowledge, discretion, instruction, teaching, commands.) Compare these words to the definitions of wisdom you developed earlier. Certainly, wisdom is the key concept contained in the book. Note that it is much more than head knowledge; it is very practical and active.

• *Where does wisdom come from?* (The source of all wisdom is God.) Point out that this same idea is found in the New Testament—in James 1:5.

• *What are some of the benefits of wisdom?* (Finding knowledge of God, victory, protection, understanding what is right and just, prolonged life, winning people's favor, riches, honor, etc.) Compare these benefits to those listed earlier.

Ask: **How can wisdom lead to prosperity and long life? How can wisdom protect us?** If no one mentions it, suggest that wisdom from God can keep us from making some foolish and life-threatening mistakes. Ask for some examples. (You may also want to point out that this isn't a guarantee that all wise people will live to be 100!)

Fear of the Lord

• *What does it mean to "fear" the Lord?* (Having a loving awe or reverence for God that involves getting to know Him and obeying His commands.) Point out that Proverbs 1:7 is sort of the motto of the whole book, so it's crucial to understand what the fear of the Lord is. You might also want to call attention to the connection between knowing and obeying God, hating evil, and fearing (or respecting) God.

• *What's the connection between wisdom and fearing God?* (Only when we care enough to really get to know God better and choose to follow His ways do we discover what true wisdom is. In this sense, the smartest scientist or Nobel prize winner in the world isn't wise if he or she never respects God enough to establish a relationship with Him.)

Summarize: **Wisdom is much more about who you know than what you know. It's more about your attitude than your aptitude!**

Have group members share any additional insights or questions they uncovered during their group study time.

Wisdom Blocks

(Needed: Paper, pencils, bricks or yellow crepe paper)

Say: **We've established that wisdom is worth pursuing and that the key thing we need to do in order to gain wisdom is to fear God—that is, get to know Him better. Simple, right?**

In theory, maybe it is simple, but not in practice. Getting to know God is a life-long process. At times it'll be an adventure; at other times it'll be a real effort.

Have kids return to the teams they formed earlier. Give each team the task of developing a list of at least five barriers to intimacy with God—things that keep us from getting to know Him better. After a few minutes, reassemble the group and have each team share its list. Spend some time as a group discussing each barrier. To make the point more memorable, you might want to use some bricks to represent each barrier. Point out that like a brick wall, these barriers can keep us from having a more intimate relationship with God. If bricks aren't available, try taping up strips of yellow crepe paper to represent a police barrier at the scene of a crime.

For each barrier, ask the following questions: **What would be some signs or symptoms of this barrier in someone's life?**

What are some specific suggestions you'd give to someone who's trying to get around this barrier?

Use the following suggestions to supplement group members' responses:

• Barrier #1—Lack of interest (apathy)

Symptoms—No priority given to prayer or Bible study, boredom with church, etc.

Suggestions—Spend some time with people who are excited about their faith, challenge God to be more real in your life, discipline yourself to pray and read the Bible for a few minutes at a time even if you don't feel like it, etc.

• Barrier #2—Lack of time

Symptoms—Involved in too many activities, high level of stress, etc.

Suggestions—Slow down, relax, spend some concentrated time alone, etc.

• Barrier #3—Unwillingness to give up a certain sin

Symptoms—Feelings of guilt or conviction, lies or deception to cover something up, etc.

Suggestions—Confession of the sin, talking with a trusted friend or counselor, etc.

• Barrier #4—Not knowing how to go about gaining wisdom

Symptoms—Feeling frustrated, not knowing where to begin, limited understanding of the Bible, etc.

Suggestions—Ask a more mature Christian to disciple you, go through a good devotional book for teens, etc.

Barrier #5—Feelings of inadequacy or unworthiness

Symptoms—Low self-esteem, constantly putting yourself down, feeling like God doesn't really care about you, etc.

Suggestions—Spend time with God anyway, share your feelings with Him, keep a journal of your thoughts and feelings, etc.

Barrier #6—Feeling that God is unapproachable or unknowable

Symptoms—Viewing God as far away and uninvolved in your daily life, never having committed to a personal relationship with Him, etc.

Suggestions—It's true that we can't fully understand God or know Him completely, but we can start by taking one small step at time. The first step might be submitting your fears and your doubts to God and starting a personal relationship with Him through acceptance of Jesus as Lord and Savior.

Barrier Breakers

(Needed: Bricks and hammer or yellow crepe paper and tape)

Have each group member choose one barrier that is most likely to interfere with his or her relationship with God. This could be something mentioned in the discussion, or something more private. Give each young person a brick (or a strip of crepe paper) to represent that barrier. In silence, have kids think of one specific step they can take this week to start overcoming that barrier.

If you're using bricks, give kids a very sturdy hammer (like a sledge hammer) and safety glasses, and let them pulverize their bricks. If you're using crepe paper, have kids tape their strips across a doorway and then break through to the other side. Either way, you'll be symbolizing the need to do something to get around (or through) the barriers that keep us from getting to know God better.

Before (or after) physically breaking through the barriers, let kids share as they are comfortable about their commitments.

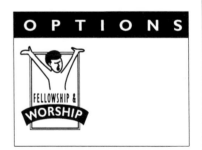

Close the session by thanking God for the fact that He wants us to get to know Him better and has taken the initiative to do that. For in Jesus Christ, we see the essence of God's Wisdom. Ask God to help you get to know Him better in our own individual ways. You could end the prayer by reading Romans 11:33 together.

STREETWISE
Wisdom Test

Circle the correct answer to each scientifically formulated question to determine how wise you really are.

1. Which of the following plants is *not* poisonous?
   a. marigold   c. sweet pea
   b. daffodil   d. lily of the valley

2. Which household appliance has the highest yearly energy cost?
   a. light bulbs throughout the entire house
   b. water heater
   c. color TV
   d. refrigerator/freezer

3. Which of the following foods has the most cholesterol?
   a. chicken (three ounces, skinless, light meat)
   b. butter (one tablespoon)
   c. ice cream (one-half cup)
   d. bacon (two slices)

4. What's the best month to buy new curtains?
   a. November   c. May
   b. August   d. February

5. What do the letters M and M stand for in M&M candies?
   a. Mercury and Mars (two planets in the Milky Way)
   b. Mars and Murrie (two head honchos at the company)
   c. More and More (from the first advertising campaign)
   d. Malt and Milk (two ingredients)

6. When was *Xmas* first used to denote Christmas?
   a. 1511 (X represents a Greek symbol for Christ)
   b. 1827 (an English abbreviation to save typesetting space)
   c. 1959 (attempt by the U.S. press to secularize the holiday)
   d. 1978 (an advertising campaign that appeared in the *New York Times*)

7. What's the traditional anniversary gift for a thirteenth-year anniversary?
   a. ivory   c. silk
   b. pottery   d. lace

8. How many miles does the average person walk in a lifetime?
   a. 6,500   c. 65,000
   b. 26,500   d. 165,000

9. How many earthworms are in a typical square acre of soil?
   a. 50,000   c. 5,000
   b. 25,000   d. 500

10. Why do pigs take mud baths?
    a. The mud destroys bacteria that causes disease in pigs.
    b. To keep cool
    c. To keep warm
    d. Pigs really don't like mud at all.

How wise are you?

10—Wise guy, eh?
9-8—Solomon's got nothing on you.
7-6—Einstein's got nothing on you.
5-4—Bozo's got nothing on you.
3-2—You're at least as wise as the guy who made up these silly questions.
0-1—Get that daffodil out of your mouth!

STREETWISE
A PROVERBS PRIMER

REPRO RESOURCE 2

PROVERB
What is a proverb? (Proverbs 1:1, 6; 10:1; 22:17; 24:23)
• A parable, saying, or riddle spoken by a wise person
• A comparison, contrast, or simile
• An analogy
• Any short saying
• Wisdom passed on from teachers who know God's laws to their students

SOLOMON
Who was Solomon?
(Proverbs 1:1; I Samuel 12:24; I Kings 3–4; I Kings 11:1-6)

Who wrote the Book of Proverbs?
(Proverbs 1:1; 10:1; 22:17-21; 24:23; 25:1; 30:1; 31:1)

WISDOM
What other words are used in the book that seem to mean something similar to wisdom? (Proverbs 1:1-8, 20, 21; 2:1, 2)

Where does wisdom come from? (Proverbs 2:6)

What are some of the benefits of wisdom? (Proverbs 2–3)

FEAR OF THE LORD
What does it mean to "fear" the Lord?
(Proverbs 1:7, 29-31; 2:1-5; 3:7; 9:10; 10:27; 14:27; 15:33; 16:6; 19:23; 31:30)

What's the connection between wisdom and fearing God? (Proverbs 1:7, 29-31; 2:1-5; 3:7; 9:10; 10:27; 14:27; 15:33; 16:6; 19:23; 31:30)

OPTIONS

SESSION ONE

Step 1

Instead of using the quiz on Repro Resource 1, stage a "Streetwise Olympics." Have kids compete in the following events:
- *Sidewalk Sidestep*—Lay out a butcher-paper path on the floor. Dot it liberally with wads of freshly-chewed chewing gum. Each person must negotiate the path in thirty seconds or less without getting gum on his or her shoes. (Adjust the time to fit the length of your "sidewalk.") Give a prize to everyone who succeeds.
- *Street Search*—Give two teams identical maps of any city. Call out the name of a street; the first team to find it wins a prize.
- *Stickup Speeches*—Have kids line up. Pretend to rob each person, one at a time, saying, **This is a stickup!** See who can give the most creative verbal response to convince you not to rob him or her. Reward the best response with a prize.

Afterward, ask: **What does it mean to be "streetwise"? Who's the most "streetwise" person you know? What other kinds of wisdom do people need?**

Step 3

Before the session, dress a group member or an adult helper as a "guru"—in a bathrobe, fake beard, etc. Hide this "wise man" somewhere in the building. Give him photocopies of the three answer sections ("Solomon," "Wisdom," and "Fear of the Lord") from the session plan. Have kids form three teams. Explain that the teams must find the wise man within two minutes (adjust according to the difficulty of the search) in order to get the photocopied answers. Those who don't find him must look up the answers.

Step 1

Make two copies of Repro Resource 1 for each group member. Have kids complete the first version according to the instructions in the session. Emphasize that kids must work alone on the sheet. (But don't give the "very naughty taxi" clue.) Before you reveal the correct answers, distribute the second version of the sheet. Explain that this time kids may work together and ask each other for the quiz answers. For instance, if you have a "flower expert" among your group members, kids might consult him or her for Question #1. After kids get opinions from other group members, they must decide whose answer to use for each question. Use this activity to make the point that wisdom involves knowing whose advice to take.

Step 3

Rather than having kids form teams to work on Repro Resource 2, give them a few minutes to look up the passages individually. However, they may *not* write down their answers. Instead, they must do their best to remember the information in the verses. After a few minutes, have kids close their Bibles. Then go through the questions on the sheet one at a time, pointing to the kids you want to answer each question. For instance, you might ask: **John, who was Solomon?** If John replies, "The son of David," ask the question to another group member—who must then give a different answer (perhaps "the king of Israel"). If a person cannot answer, he or she is out. Continue until you have all the answers you're looking for for each question.

Step 1

As group members arrive, seat them as though they're about to take their SAT exams. Space the kids apart as much as possible, give them each a #2 pencil, have them remain quiet, etc. When everyone is seated, explain that instead of taking the SAT in the traditional manner, kids will be working as teams on the exam. Have kids form three teams (the "S Team," the "A Team," and the "T Team"). You will ask a series of nearly impossible questions. After you ask a question, team members will consult together to answer it. When a team comes up with an answer, one of its members must run to the board and write it down. The first team to write the correct answer gets a point. The team with the most points at the end of the game is the winner. If possible, try to make your questions so hard that only one or two is likely to be answered. Then for your final question, ask: **What is wisdom?** Use this activity to lead into a discussion on the difference between knowledge and wisdom.

Step 3

Before the session, write each of the questions on Repro Resource 2 on a separate sheet of poster board. Then post the signs in various places around the room. You'll also need to write each of the Scripture references listed on the sheet on a separate index card. Distribute the index cards to your group members (one card per person). Instruct kids to look up their assigned passage, decide which question it applies to, and stand under the appropriate sign. Then have the members of each newly formed group under each sign fully answer their question. After a few minutes, have each group share its findings.

OPTIONS

SESSION ONE

Step 2
Kids may think of biblical "wisdom" as something for old people. Like many people in our culture, they may value what current celebrities say over what an old Book says. Share the following examples of celebrity "wisdom": **"I will not change. When you are successful and you change, you are an idiot"**—Arnold Schwarzenegger. "I watch [the movie *Heaven Can Wait*] constantly because it causes me to re-explore my values. I hope I can act half as cool as Warren Beatty in the years to come"—Dr. Dré, rap star. "My expression for the '90s is 'stash the cash.' I'm not willing to sell my very soul—but almost"—Daniel J. Travanti, actor. "Every time I perform, I have to have it [a "lucky" ring she's worn since tenth grade] on. If I can't wear it around my neck, I'll put it around my waist"—Mariah Carey, singer. "People who believe in voodoo are as serious as people who believe in any other religion. Making fun of zombies comes out of ignorance"—Cicely Tyson, actress. Ask: **How wise are these statements? Doesn't the wisdom of the Bible deserve at least equal time?**

Step 3
Kids may think of Proverbs as irrelevant—a bunch of sayings that are either obvious or don't make any sense, about as useful as the messages in fortune cookies. Help them to see the book as the hard-won insights of a lifetime, shared out of concern for the reader. Say: **Pretend that you have only two minutes to live, and must pass along to your children two of the most important things you've learned in life.** Give group members two minutes to write; then share results. Ask: **If you really had to do this, how would you want people to treat what you'd written?**

Step 3
If your kids aren't familiar with the Bible, they may have a hard time answering the questions on Repro Resource 2. So instead of having kids form teams to work on the sheet, work on it together as a group. You may even want to turn the activity into a game. Help your group members find the Book of Proverbs in their Bibles. Before you ask each question, write the accompanying passages on the board. Go through the questions one at a time, giving kids an opportunity to look up the passages and shout out the answers. The first person to shout out a correct answer gets a point. There's more than one correct answer for each question, so there are several points available. After you've gone through all of the questions, you may want to award a prize to the person with the most points.

Step 4
Kids with little Bible background may have difficulty brainstorming barriers to intimacy with God. So rather than having kids form teams to come up with barriers, try a different approach. Have kids form pairs. Assign each pair one of the barriers listed in the session. Also read some of the symptoms associated with each barrier, as well as suggestions for overcoming the barrier. Then have the pairs come up with some potential problems kids might face in applying the suggestions to the barrier problem. (For instance, one of the suggestions for "Barrier #1—Lack of interest [apathy]" is "Spend some time with people who are excited about their faith." One potential problem is that some kids don't know anyone who is excited about his or her faith.) After a few minutes, have each pair share what it came up with. You'll want to be prepared to offer some workable solutions to the problems the pairs name.

Step 1
After completing Repro Resource 1, have each group member come up with one more trivia question that only he or she will know the answer to. One at a time, have each person ask his or her question. Then give the rest of the group ten seconds to answer it. After all group members have asked their questions, say: **We're all knowledgeable in different areas. Likewise, we're probably all wise in different areas.** Point out that God imparts different kinds of wisdom to people. So a good way to make maximum use of God's imparted wisdom is to seek advice from each other. Help your group members see that they're a team when it comes to gaining wisdom.

Step 5
Distribute file folders and pencils to your group members. Explain that the folders are to be used as "faith files." Instruct kids to write in their folders any answered prayers or fulfilled needs they've experienced from God. Give kids a few minutes to begin their files. Afterward, ask volunteers to share some of their faith-building memories. Then say: **Add to your folder every time God comes through for you or every time you overcome one of the barriers we just identified. Then, whenever you feel like you just can't get over the next hurdle in your way, you can pull out this file and be reminded of all the times you and God have done it together before.**

OPTIONS

SESSION ONE

Step 2
Ask for a couple of volunteers to help you perform a skit. Explain that you will play the role of a popular, good-looking guy in school. One of the volunteers will play the role of the most beautiful girl in school. The other girl will play the role of the smartest—and wisest—girl in school. Explain that you will perform the skit twice. The first time, you (the popular, good-looking guy) will talk to the beautiful girl and ignore the other one, even though both girls are vying for your attention. The second time, you will talk to smart (and wise) girl and ignore the beautiful one. See how both girls react to being talked to and ignored. Afterward, ask your girls which version of the skit they think is most realistic. Ask: **Do you think most guys care about how wise a girl is? Why or why not? If not, what other benefits are there to being wise?**

Step 4
Have your group members imagine that a new girl has arrived at school. She seems nice, and has indicated that she'd like to make friends. Ask your group members to make a list of five reasons or "obstacles" that might prevent them from becoming friends with this girl. You might throw out some examples like "My other friends might get jealous" or "I'm too busy." After a few minutes, have your group members read their lists. Use this activity to lead in to a discussion on building a relationship with God, and the barriers that can make this difficult.

Step 1
Begin the meeting dressed as "The Great Wise One"—perhaps wearing robe, fake beard, and turban. Say: **I am so wise, I know the answers to questions that haven't even been asked. Let me show you.** [NOTE: This is very similar to Johnny Carson's old "Carnac" routine.] Before the session, prepare several envelopes, each with a question sealed inside and three answers written on the outside. Hold up each envelope to your forehead, concentrate, and announce the three answers. Then open the envelope and read the question. This activity is designed to be humorous, and will work best if you include the names of your group members in the answers. For example, you might give the following answers: **Double-pump, two-handed reverse slam; Porky Pig; and _____** (the name of a guy in your group who thinks he's pretty cool). You would then open the envelope and read: **What is a dunk, a chunk, and a punk?** Try to use enough questions so that each of your guys is mentioned (and poked fun at lightheartedly) at least once.

Step 2
Focus on the key words *knowledge*, *insight*, and *judgment*. Ask: **How might these three things apply to someone who wants to become a good basketball player?** (Knowledge comes from listening to what the coach says in practice. Insight comes from watching how other basketball players play. Judgment comes from making decisions on the court.) Then ask: **How might these three things apply to someone who wants to improve his Bible study time?** (Knowledge comes from reading the Bible and listening to what other Christians say about it. Insight comes from asking, "What does this passage mean to me?" Judgment comes from applying the Bible to life situations.)

Step 1
To begin the session, play "Wisdom Bingo." Before the session, prepare several cards. Write the letters W-I-S-D-O-M across the top of each card. Under each letter, draw a vertical column of six boxes. Use increments of 12 for the numbers in each column (W = 1-12; I = 13-24; S = 25-36; D = 37-48; O = 49-60; M = 61-72). Write the appropriate numbers randomly on each card. Then prepare small slips of paper to "draw" during the game. For the most part, the game is played just like regular Bingo. (Of course, when someone covers a row of numbers, he or she should yell "Wisdom!") However, when someone calls out "Wisdom!" he or she hasn't automatically won the game. At that point, you will ask him or her a Trivial Pursuit question (allowing the player to choose the category). If the person answers it correctly, he or she wins. If not, he or she is out, and the game continues.

Step 2
Have kids form teams. Explain that there are slips of paper with the letters W, I, S, D, O, and M written on them (one set for each team) hidden in six places around the church. You will use Bible verses as clues. These verses should tie in with the different hiding places ("I stand at the door and knock" [Revelation 3:20]—church entrance; "Sing to the Lord a new song" [Psalm 149:1]—choir loft, "I am the bread of life" [John 6:48]—kitchen; "Jesus was baptized too" [Luke 3:21]—baptistry; etc.) Give each team a clue to start with. Each hiding place should have six slips of paper (one for each team) that have one of the letters written on them, as well as six other Bible-verse clues (one for each team) that will help the teams find the next hiding place. The first team to return all six letters to you is the winner.

OPTIONS

SESSION ONE

MEDIA

Step 1
Using a VCR and monitor, show scenes (which you've pre-screened) featuring some of the following movie "wise men"—characters who share their "wisdom" with others: Ten Bears (*Dances with Wolves*), Obi-Wan Kenobi (*Star Wars*), Yoda (*The Empire Strikes Back*), Gandhi (*Gandhi*), Humphrey Bogart's ghost (*Play It Again, Sam*), Mr. Miyagi (*The Karate Kid*), and Gordon Gekko (*Wall Street*). Then discuss the scenes, using the following questions: **How are these "wise men" similar? How are they different? Which do you think are really wise? Why? If you were going to ask advice from a "wise man"—or woman—what would you want that person to be like?**

Step 4
Show the following scenes from *The Wizard of Oz* on video. First, about two-thirds of the way through the film, Dorothy and her friends approach the fearsome, fiery Oz and ask for things they need (courage, brains, etc.). Ask: **Is this what it's like to ask God for wisdom? Why or why not?** Second, near the end of the movie, the all-too-human Oz presents the Scarecrow and others with substitutes for what they seek. Ask: **If the Scarecrow had asked for wisdom instead of brains, what do you think he would have gotten? Is this how God deals with requests for wisdom? Explain.**

SHORT MEETING TIME

Step 1
Name some pairs of characters from TV shows. Have kids vote on which character in each pair is wiser. Here are some pairs you might use: Will (*Fresh Prince of Bel-Air*) or Martin (*Martin*); Roseanne Connor (*Roseanne*) or Dr. Quinn (*Dr. Quinn, Medicine Woman*); Bart Simpson or Lisa Simpson (*The Simpsons*); Commander Benjamin Sisko (*Deep Space Nine*) or Captain Jean-Luc Picard (*Star Trek: The Next Generation*). Afterward, ask: **How did you decide who was wiser? Are there different kinds of wisdom? What are wise people able to accomplish that others can't?**

Step 3
Summarize yourself the definition of *proverb* and who Solomon was. Then ask the following questions, having kids look for answers in the accompanying passages. **Where does wisdom come from?** (Proverbs 2:6.) **What are some benefits of wisdom?** (Proverbs 3.) Read Proverbs 9:10. Explain that fearing the Lord is having a loving awe and reverence for Him. It includes knowing and obeying Him. To save more time, replace Steps 4 and 5 with the following. Read II Chronicles 1:1, 6-12. Ask: **What kind of relationship did Solomon have with God before he asked for wisdom? What did Solomon get? Why do you think God was so pleased?** To help kids consider why they need wisdom, have volunteers tell how they might have completed the sentence from verse 10: "Give me wisdom and knowledge, that I may . . ." To close, have the group brainstorm at least eight areas in which kids might need wisdom (choice of colleges and careers, study habits, picking friends, getting along with parents, buying things, etc.). Then have each person list these in the order in which he or she feels the greatest need.

URBAN

Step 1
To give Repro Resource 1 an urban slant, add the following question:
• **A recent study in Boston found that gang members would be willing to give up selling drugs if they could be guaranteed to make how much money per hour?**
a. $8-10
b. $12-17
c. $20-25
d. $26-30
(The answer is a.)

Step 2
If your kids live in a world in which mere survival is an everyday concern, they may question the importance of striving after wisdom. So you'll need to help them recognize that wisdom can be beneficial to them in their daily lives. As a group, brainstorm a list of ways in which wisdom can help an inner-city teenager. Among other things, wisdom can help a young person sort out his or her future, allowing him or her to recognize which paths are "dead ends" and which lead to opportunity. Wisdom might also help a young person keep his or her head when faced with a difficult situation (like a gang confrontation). Wisdom might help a young person find a suitable mate in a society inundated with sexual immorality. After you've established some of the potential benefits of wisdom, lead in to a discussion on how to *gain* wisdom.

OPTIONS

SESSION ONE

Step 1
The questions on Repro Resource 1 are pretty obscure and trivial. It's not likely that your high schoolers will know more of the answers than your junior highers do. Therefore, a game based on this quiz might work well for a mixed group. Have kids form a circle with their chairs. Ask each quiz question one at a time. But instead of giving all four possible answer choices, give only two (the correct one and another one). Instruct kids to *physically* answer each question. They should move one seat to the left if they choose "A," and one seat to the right if they choose "B." After everyone has moved, give the correct answer. Those who answered correctly are still in; those who didn't are out. (And those who have someone sitting on their lap probably *wish* they were out!) Continue until only one person remains. Then crown him or her the "Wise Old Owl." (You might want to award him or her something scholarly, like a notebook or ruler.)

Step 2
Ask each of your junior highers to make a list of situations he or she has faced (or is facing) that required some degree of wisdom. Their lists might include things like an important choice, a response to someone, an attitude change, etc. Ask each of your high schoolers to make a list of the costs they've "paid" in becoming wiser. Their lists might include things like friends who they think they're weird for making wise choices, a lack of popularity for not following the crowd, less free time, etc. After a few minutes, have the kids in each age group share their lists. Then ask your high schoolers to share whether or not they think the "costs" of their wise choices were "worth it."

Step 1
Have your kids form pairs. Then distribute lists of questions for members of each pair to ask each other. The lists should include questions like "How many freckles do you have on your body?" "How tall will you be when you stop growing?" "What did you do on the afternoon of March 21, 1984?" "How many hairs fell out of your head the last time you used a hairbrush or comb?" Of course kids won't know the answers to these questions; but have them try to make educated guesses. Then have someone read aloud Matthew 10:30 to give kids a sense of the scope of God's knowledge. Briefly discuss whether knowledge and wisdom are the same thing. Ask: **If you knew the answers to all of the questions we asked earlier, would that make you wise?** (Not necessarily.) Point out that God is both ultimately knowledgeable and fully wise. Ask: **If you were all knowing, all wise, and all loving, wouldn't you want to give some of that wisdom to those you loved? God does. And that's partly what Proverbs is for.**

Step 2
Ask group members to brainstorm some common sayings, phrases, or terms that mention wisdom. List these on the board as they are named. Kids may mention things like "Wise as an owl"; "streetwise"; "Early to bed, early to rise makes a man healthy, wealthy, and wise"; "wisdom teeth"; "wisecracks"; etc. After you've compiled a list, ask: **What do these phrases and terms suggest about the nature of wisdom?** (It comes with age; it involves humor; it is part of moderate living; etc.) Then explain: **As we look at the Book of Proverbs, we will discover what wisdom is really all about!**

Date Used:

Approx. Time

Step 1: Who's the Wisest of Them All? _____
o Extra Action
o Small Group
o Large Group
o Fellowship & Worship
o Mostly Guys
o Extra Fun
o Media
o Short Meeting Time
o Urban
o Combined Jr. High/High School
o Extra Challenge

Step 2: What Is Wisdom? _____
o Heard It All Before
o Mostly Girls
o Mostly Guys
o Extra Fun
o Urban
o Combined Jr. High/High School
o Extra Challenge

Step 3: A Proverbs Primer _____
o Extra Action
o Small Group
o Large Group
o Heard It All Before
o Little Bible Background
o Short Meeting Time

Step 4: Wisdom Blocks _____
o Little Bible Background
o Mostly Girls
o Media

Step 5: Barrier Breakers _____
o Fellowship & Worship

SESSION 2
A Fool and His Happiness Are Soon Parted

YOUR GOALS FOR THIS SESSION:
Choose one or more

☐ To help kids identify different types of foolishness.

☐ To help kids understand the importance of avoiding foolish ways.

☐ To help kids evaluate their own ways to determine how wise or foolish they have been lately, and commit to seeking after wisdom.

☐ Other _____

Your Bible Base:

Selected Proverbs

CUSTOM CURRICULUM

Fooling Around

(Needed: Chalkboard and chalk or newsprint and marker, April Fool's novelties [optional])

Before the meeting, write "A fool is . . ." on the board. As kids arrive, distribute chalk or markers and instruct them to write down how they would complete the sentence.

To get kids in the mood, you might want to bring in some typical "April Fool's" novelties—fake vomit, rubber noses, etc. While kids complete the sentence starter and examine the novelties, begin a discussion with some general questions about foolishness.

Ask: **What's the best April Fool's joke you've ever played or heard of?** Let kids share their stories. You may want to supplement their responses with the following ideas (from the author's college days): smearing black shoe polish on black toilet seats, putting Vaseline on doorknobs so that the doors can't be opened, tying a rope between two opposing doors, so that neither can be opened, a teacher giving an extremely difficult pop quiz on which the final question is "What day is today?"

Why do some people enjoy April Fool's pranks? Get a few responses.

When can a joke backfire, or do more harm than good? (When someone gets hurt, embarrassed, or made fun of.)

What is a fool, anyway? Read off some of the group members' responses from the board. Then point out that one dictionary definition of a fool is "a person lacking judgment or prudence." Some synonyms listed in the dictionary include idiot, imbecile, moron, and simpleton.

No one wants to be considered a fool. What kinds of people would kids your age say are most foolish? Why? Encourage a variety of answers. Some young people may say that kids who blow off school are foolish. Others may say that kids who don't party a lot are foolish. Some may say that kids who engage in "unsafe" sex are foolish. Others may say that virgins are foolish. Some may say that parents or other authority figures are fools.

What kinds of people do you think the Bible says are most foolish? Get responses from several group members. Then point out that the Book of Proverbs has a lot to say about fools. Much of the book contrasts wisdom and folly. That's what you're going to look at today.

31

STEP 2

Fool House

(Needed: Copies of Repro Resource 3, pencils)

Hand out copies of "Fool House" (Repro Resource 3) and pencils. Instruct group members to complete the sheet individually or in small groups. When everyone is finished, have group members share their responses.

Start by having kids call out some of the last names they came up with for each character. After group members have shared the names they came up with, suggest the following ones: Alexis Adulteress, Wanda Wise, Samantha Simple, Francis Fool, Molly Mocker, and Sally Sluggard. (The significance of these names will become more obvious in the next step.)

Next, have group members share their rankings. Obviously, kids will say that Wanda is the wisest; but how did they rank the rest? There's no one right way, but you might want to suggest the following order based on the severity or harmfulness of each: Wanda, Samantha, Sally, Francis, Molly, and Alexis.

Give group members a few minutes to explain why they ranked the characters as they did. Then move on to the Bible study, in which you'll look at some verses to describe each type of character.

STEP 3

Fool Proof

(Needed: Bibles, chalkboard and chalk or newsprint and marker)

Say: **In this session, we're going to be looking at different types of people described in the Book of Proverbs. These people include The Wise, The Simple, The Fool, The Mocker, The Adulteress, and The Sluggard.** List these names on the board as you mention them.

CUSTOM CURRICULUM

OPTIONS

You'll study the first type of person—The Wise—as a group. Instruct group members to open their Bibles to Proverbs. Have them skim through the book randomly, calling out any characteristics of a wise person they find. (This activity could also serve as a review of the first session.) Here are some characteristics your group members may find:

The Wise
• Fear the Lord (Proverbs 1:7).
• Listen to instruction (1:8).
• Don't give in to sin (1:10).

After your group members have come up with several characteristics of The Wise, have them form teams to study the rest of the types of people listed on the board. Assign each team one or more of the types on the board, as well as the accompanying passages to look up. Instruct each team to answer these two questions:
• **What do these passages say about this type of person?**
• **What are two or three modern-day examples of someone exhibiting this type of behavior?**
Use the following information to guide your discussion of the activity.

The Simple (Proverbs 1:22; 9:1-6, 13-18; 14:15, 18)
• *Description*—A simple person is someone who is easily persuaded or lacks good judgment. Other words for "simple" might include "gullible" or "naive." In many ways, all people start out as "simple" and have to choose whether they will follow the way of wisdom or the way of folly. Some simple people enjoy being simple, thinking ignorance is bliss.
• *Examples*—Someone who engages in immoral sexual activity, but doesn't realize it's immoral; someone who is curious about spiritual things and is willing to try anything, even cults.
Ask: **In Proverbs 9, both wisdom and folly call out to simple people. How are their invitations similar and different? Why do some people choose folly over wisdom?** (Both want simple people to come into her "house" or way of life. Wisdom has done more advance preparation. Wisdom demands leaving simple ways behind. Folly's feast consists of stolen water and food that is so shameful it can only be eaten in secret. Sinful pleasures might "taste" good for a moment, but they won't provide any lasting enjoyment.)

The Fool (Proverbs 1:7, 22; 12:15, 16; 13:19; 26:11; 28:26)
• *Description*—A fool is someone who knows the difference between right and wrong but deliberately chooses wrong. Fools don't want to be told how they should live. They shun other people's advice if it contradicts what they want to do. Fools repeat their foolishness (sin), even though they have enough knowledge or experience to know better.
• *Examples*—Someone who knows the dangers of drinking and

driving, but does so anyway; someone who has read about the dangers of steroids, but chooses to use them anyway in order to look better.

Ask: **Can a smart person be foolish? If so, how? Why do some people deliberately choose to repeat "foolish" behavior?** (Intelligence, as measured by IQ or SAT tests, has nothing to do with whether someone is wise or foolish. Wisdom involves someone's willingness to learn God's ways and apply what's learned in daily life.)

As you talk about the repeat nature of foolishness, you might want to have kids compare Proverbs 26:11 with Proverbs 23:29-35. The verses in chapter 23 talk about one specific type of foolishness—alcohol abuse. It's a very accurate portrayal of drunkenness. Note the last part of verse 35, where the drunk wants to wake up only to have another drink. Harmful behaviors like drunkenness, sexual immorality, drug abuse, and the like can become addictive. These behaviors might give some short-term pleasure, but the cycle is extremely destructive as the person caught in it always needs to find a greater thrill or high in order to get the same level of pleasure. Give kids an opportunity to talk about addictions, and follow up outside of your group time with any who want to talk more about it.

The Mocker (Proverbs 1:22; 13:1; 15:12; 21:24; 22:10; 29:8)
• *Description*—A mocker is someone who makes fun of others, especially those who are following wisdom. Mockers are arrogant and don't want to be corrected. They delight in putting others down. Because of their insults and their intent to cause harm, mockers cause quarrels and strife between others.
• *Examples*—Someone who teases others who choose not to drink; someone who enjoys putting down people of other races.

Ask: **Why would someone delight in mockery?** (It sets the person up in a position of superiority. His or her acquaintances might try to get on the person's good side so as not to become the brunt of his or her offensive remarks. The person's mockery might make him or her feel somewhat better about his or her own foolishness.)

The Adulteress (Proverbs 2:16-19; 5:3-6; 6:24; 7:4, 5, 21-23; 22:14)
• *Description*—In Proverbs, the adulteress is depicted as an unfaithful wife intentionally trying to lead impressionable young men into her trap by seducing them. Though she can be awfully tempting, those who give in to her find death, not life. The adulteress can also be taken symbolically to represent any person who intentionally tries to get someone else to engage in immoral behavior, including, but not limited to, sexual immorality. In this sense, the adulteress could be an individual (male or female), or even a group. Note that Proverbs seems to be suggesting a progression in which each succeeding character is more dangerous. Someone starts out simple. He or she chooses whether to follow wisdom or folly. Those who choose folly become foolish. Those who

are deeply into their foolish ways begin teasing or mocking those who aren't. Those who are most completely entrenched in their foolishness actively try to recruit or trap others to join them in their sinful ways. Misery loves company.

• *Examples*—Obvious examples would include prostitutes and drug dealers. The list could also include peers who pressure others into engaging in immoral behavior, a guy pressuring his date to have sex, or even advertisers who try to "seduce" others into buying something they don't need.

Say: **Proverbs 2:19 says, "None who go to her [the adulteress] return or attain the paths of life." Does this mean that there's no turning back for someone who has committed adultery or other immoral behavior? Why or why not?** (Obviously, the rest of Scripture depicts a loving God who can rescue us from any type of sinful, immoral behavior. Yet anyone who deliberately and repeatedly chooses to give in to immoral behavior is playing with fire. It's not that God can't still save the person; it's that the person may get to a point where he or she no longer senses any need for God.)

The Sluggard (Proverbs 6:6-11; 10:26; 13:4; 21:25; 24:30-34)

• *Description*—A sluggard is a lazy person who doesn't want to work for the things he or she craves. Others find such people very irritating. The sluggard appears many times throughout the Book of Proverbs and seems to be a special type of fool that the writers have singled out. Many times the sluggard is depicted in some type of humorous fashion.

• *Examples*—Someone who has the ability, but refuses to study in order to improve his or her grades; someone who refuses to work but would rather take advantage of someone else's generosity.

Ask: **Without naming names, who's the laziest person you know? Why do you think this person is so lazy?** Don't dwell very long on this. Try to get kids thinking about the source of laziness. For some, it's just a matter of taking advantage of others so that they don't have to work as hard. Ask kids to comment on Proverbs 10:26. Get them to comment on why lazy people can be so irritating.

STEP 4

What Kind of Fool Am I?

(Needed: Copies of Repro Resource 4, one of which is cut apart)

Before the session, you'll need to cut apart one copy of "What Kind of Fool Am I?" (Repro Resource 4). At this point in the session, distribute complete copies of Repro Resource 4 so that group members can see the six categories. Note that "The Adulteress" has been renamed "The Tempter" so as to include both genders. Ask for two volunteers to come forward. Have each volunteer draw one of the cards from the cut-apart copy of Repro Resource 4. You will set up a situation. Each volunteer will then answer questions that you and/or other group members pose as if he or she was the type of person indicated on the card. After several questions have been posed, see if group members can guess what type of person the volunteer is pretending to be. As time allows, ask for additional volunteers for each of the other situations.

Here are the situations and possible questions:

Situation 1: You have a major test at school tomorrow.
• **How did you study for the test?**
• **What is your strategy for passing the test?**
• **What did you say to your classmates after taking the test?**

Situation 2: Several kids are talking about the big party that's going to take place Friday night at the Johnsons'— while Mr. and Mrs. Johnson are out of town.
• **Are you going to the party?**
• **What are you saying about the party?**
• **How do you feel inside as people are talking about the party?**

Situation 3: You're home alone and an R-rated movie you're not supposed to watch is showing on one of the cable channels.
• **Do you watch it?**
• **If so, why? If not, why not?**
• **A friend calls just as you're deciding what to watch. What do you say to this friend?**

Feel free to come up with additional situations if you have time. Some possibilities might include sitting at the lunch table with a group of people making fun of the class "nerds" or talking with a group of friends about a classmate who is HIV-positive.

Some of your volunteers may have difficulty with this activity, because they may not know how to respond to some of the questions. That's OK. Let them struggle with it a bit. You want to get them thinking about what it would mean to be wise or foolish in a variety of situations. Getting them to think about this in a general sense will help prepare them to make specific application of the Scripture in their own lives.

Beyond Folly

(Needed: Copies of Repro Resource 4, pencils, scissors [optional])

Refer to the six types of people listed on "What Kind of Fool Am I?" (Repro Resource 4). Point out that an understanding of these people will help your kids get more out of the Book of Proverbs if they study it on their own in the future. Have kids cut apart the six cards on the sheet and write down the following lists on the back of each card:

The Wise—List one or more areas of your life in which you feel the need for more wisdom.

The Simple—List three advantages of seeking after God's wisdom in your life.

The Fool—List one or more foolish things you've done lately.

The Mocker—List one or more things you could say to someone who teases you for choosing wisdom over something foolish.

The Tempter—List three things that tempt you most, or three situations in which you feel most tempted.

The Sluggard—List any areas of your life in which you are especially lazy or could be lazy if you allowed yourself to be.

After kids have given some thought to these lists, have them get into groups of three to share their responses to at least one card. If your kids are comfortable praying together, let each group spend some time in prayer. If some kids aren't ready for that, you could say the closing prayer. You might want to structure your closing prayer around Ephesians 1:17-23.

S T R E E T W I S E

FOOL HOUSE

REPRO RESOURCE
3

THE SETTING
A sorority party during pledge week at the University.

THE CHARACTERS
• **Alexis.** When the party is in full swing, she brings out some crack cocaine and all of the necessary paraphernalia to smoke it. She says that this is the *real* initiation ceremony—and all those who don't participate are fools.

• **Wanda.** Since she wants to be Alexis' friend, she's tempted to try it—but she knows that would be stupid. She says, "I'm not into that stuff," and leaves the party.

• **Samantha.** She's never tried crack and doesn't know much about it. She says, "I'll try anything once," thinking it might be something like a peace pipe.

• **Francis.** She's heard that crack is dangerous and should be avoided. She's gotten lectures about it at home, church, even school. She knows she's supposed to "just say no," but she wants to fit in, so she smokes it anyway.

• **Molly.** She smokes some herself. As she does, she gives Wanda a hard time about not joining in, calling her "little miss goody two-shoes" and some other names that can't be repeated here.

• **Sally.** Sally was supposed to attend the party, but she took a late afternoon nap and overslept. When she finally showed up, the party was over.

Give a last name to each character that describes her behavior. Try to use a word that starts with the same letter as her first name. Then rank the characters from 1 to 6, with "1" being the wisest and "6" being the most foolish.

		Rank
Alexis	_____	_____
Wanda	_____	_____
Samantha	_____	_____
Francis	_____	_____
Molly	_____	_____
Sally	_____	_____

S T R E E T W I S E

What Kind of Fool Am I?

REPRO RESOURCE 4

The Wise

The Simple

The Fool

The Mocker

The Tempter

The Sluggard

OPTIONS

SESSION TWO

Step 1
Have kids compete to see who can look the most foolish. Provide orange slices with the rind still on them (for kids to hold in their mouths while smiling); Chiclets gum (to be used as big teeth that stick out); wax lips; Ping-Pong balls cut in half and markers (to make goofy eyeballs); and slices of bologna (to be used as tongues that hang out). Have hairbrushes and styling gel available for the truly foolhardy. Take Polaroid photos of contestants at their most foolish. Then post the photos for judging by the group or by a couple of impartial guests. Award a prize to the winner, and let kids keep their photos. Then ask: **Does a foolish person always look foolish? Explain.**

Step 3
Have volunteers play the roles of five hospital patients—The Simple, The Fool, The Mocker, The Adulteress, and The Sluggard. They should keep their characters' identities secret, however. Have the actors take their places around the room, acting as their characters would, lying on "hospital beds" (short rows of chairs placed together). Tape a "chart"—a sheet of paper on which you've written Bible references from Step 3 of the session—to each bed. You will play the role of the wise old doctor who's taking interns (the rest of the group) on rounds through the ward. As you come to each bed, observe the "symptoms" of the patient and have interns describe them. Then have the interns read the verses and give a "diagnosis" (tell which type of person the patient is). Afterward, discuss the activity, using the questions from the session.

Step 3
Assign one of the characters on Repro Resource 3 to each of your group members. (Change the names and genders of the characters as needed.) Instruct each group member to write a summary of the events of the party (described on Repro Resource 3)—from the point of view of his or her character. For instance, "Alexis" might explain why she decided to bring out the crack pipe and how she felt about the other characters' reactions. "Wanda" might explain what she thought when she first saw the crack pipe and how she felt when she left the party. After a few minutes, have each person read his or her account.

Step 5
Assign each group member one of the lists to tackle on his or her own. Make your assignments according to the characters you assigned in Step 3 (see above). For instance, you'll give "The Wise" assignment to the person who wrote from Wanda's point of view in Step 3; you'll give "The Simple" assignment to the person who wrote from Samantha's point of view; etc. Give group members a few minutes to work on their lists. When everyone is finished, ask each person to share at least one item from his or her list with the rest of the group.

Step 2
Have your kids form groups of six. Distribute copies of Repro Resource 3. Instruct group members to read the situation on the sheet. Then have each group come up with a new scenario based on a similar situation. However, instead of being tempted by crack cocaine, the people in the skit might be faced with drinking alcohol, sneaking into an adult party club, cheating on a test, vandalizing a building, spreading vicious rumors, etc. The characters in the new scenario may have different names (perhaps the names of the members of the group), but they should respond in the same way that the various characters on Repro Resource 3 responded. After a few minutes, have each group read aloud its new scenario.

Step 3
Have kids form six groups. Assign each group one of the "types" of people listed in the session. Give each group a large sheet of newsprint and a black marker. Within each group, have members appoint "researchers" (to look up the Bible passages), "recorders" (to write down the information), and "relevance seekers" (to apply the information to modern-day situations). Have each group make a large poster, with the "type" of person printed at the top and the rest of the information written below. As time permits, group members may also draw pictures of types of people who fit their category. After a few minutes, have each group share its findings and display its poster.

OPTIONS

SESSION TWO

HEARD IT ALL BEFORE

Step 2
If the "Fool House" scenario and the made-up names are too clichéd or hokey for your kids, try another option. Bring newspaper and magazine clippings about risky activities (car racing, missionary work, running for office, starting a business, drug dealing, drug use, being a police officer, riding an amusement park ride, drinking alcohol, making fun of spiritual things, joining a gang, working as a telephone solicitor, teaching in the inner city, sexual promiscuity, buying a lottery ticket, etc.). Have kids try to arrange the clippings in order of the foolishness involved in taking the risks—from least foolish to most foolish. Allow no more than five minutes for this. Then discuss the difficulty of comparing some risks, and ask kids to explain why they felt certain activities were more foolish than others.

Step 5
"Heard it all before" kids are likely to be mockers who think themselves wise. They'll probably resist the self-criticism called for in the session's conclusion. Instead, have them form pairs. Explain that one partner is wise, and the other is a mocker. The wise partner will try to walk across the room. The mocker can force him or her to stop every few seconds and take a step backward by mocking him or her. The wise person may then resume walking. Eventually the wise partner will make it across the room. When all of the wise partners reach the other side of the room, reveal that you neglected to mention an important fact: The mockers' side of the room was on fire. The mockers may have been clever "wiseguys," but the wise people made it to safety. Use this to illustrate the fact that in order to make progress at anything, including a relationship with God, it's necessary to stop mocking and start moving.

LITTLE BIBLE BACKGROUND

Step 2
Kids with little Bible background aren't likely to come up with last names like "Adulteress," "Mocker," and "Sluggard" for the characters on Repro Resource 3. In fact, they may have a hard time even understanding the assignment. So rather than having kids work on the sheet individually or in small groups, go through the information as an entire group. Bring six people to the front of the room. Assign each person one of the identities on Repro Resource 3. (Change the genders and names of the characters as necessary.) Read the information on the sheet, directing the actions of each character as you do. For instance, when you read that Wanda "leaves the party," you might escort the person playing Wanda out the door of your room. Afterward, have your six "actors" stand in front of the group. Then have the rest of your group members rank them from 1 to 6 according to who was wisest.

Step 5
If your group members don't have much experience applying biblical principles to their lives, they may have some problems coming up with personal lists for each card on Repro Resource 4. Instead, you might want to brainstorm some items for each list as a group. For instance, for "The Wise," you might ask: **What are some areas in which kids your age may feel they need more wisdom?** List group members' responses on the board. Once you have a sizable list for each category, have group members choose the items that apply to them and write them on their cards.

FELLOWSHIP & WORSHIP

Step 1
Have your group members brainstorm a list of the various things God has given us to help keep us from being fools. List the items on the board as group members name them. The list might include things like the Bible, parents, natural intelligence, school, other Christians, godly advice columnists, etc. Then lead the group in a brief prayer of thanks to God for His goodness and love, and for "arming" us to recognize and avoid the wily ways of the world.

Step 5
Have your kids form groups of three. Instruct each group to write its own proverb about being foolish and wise in ways that pertain to modern-day situations. ("My son, give not yourself to an abundance of television; for in the multitude of shows, there is foolishness.") After a few minutes, have each group share its proverb.

OPTIONS

S E S S I O N   T W O

MOSTLY GIRLS

MOSTLY GUYS

EXTRA FUN

Mostly Girls

Step 2
After group members complete Repro Resource 3, point out that all of the characters on the sheet are female. Ask: **If this story were about a guys' frat party, how might some of the characters' actions be different?** Depending on the guys your group members know, your girls may say that if the characters had been guys, probably none of them would have done what Wanda did. Or they may say that more than one of them would have overslept and missed the party like Sally did. Briefly discuss how guys and girls might respond differently to situations like the one on Repro Resource 3.

Step 5
After your group members complete their lists, have them sit together in a circle. Hand a candle (or flashlight) to one of the girls. Ask her to share something from one of her cards that she would appreciate prayer for. Then have her pass the candle to the person on her right. That person will then pray for the first girl and share something from one of *her* cards. Then she will pass the candle to her right, and so on. Continue until everyone in the circle has shared. Then as you wrap up the session, point out that making wise decisions involves supportive friends.

Mostly Guys

Step 1
Continue the discussion on foolishness by asking your group members to name some foolish things that high school guys sometimes do. If your guys are reluctant to respond, suggest things like unwise sexual behavior (going farther than you know is right), drinking, smoking, cheating, fighting, etc. Briefly discuss what makes each action unwise, focusing particularly on the negative consequences of each one.

Step 4
Put together or purchase a video "highlight" clip of foolish moments in sports history. (For instance, you might show Michigan's Chris Webber calling time out at the end of the 1993 NCAA basketball championship game—when his team didn't have any time outs left.) You could show clips of poor decisions in football games, baseball games, motorbike racing, downhill skiing, etc. Afterward, point out that most of us have "20-20 hindsight." In other words, it's easy to look back on our past actions and recognize the foolish choices we made. However, at that point, it's often too late to escape the consequences. Emphasize that we need to seek wisdom from God to *prevent* ourselves from making foolish choices.

Extra Fun

Step 1
Begin the session with a "fish toss." You'll need a large, greased (perhaps with Vaseline), whole fish in an appropriately sized bucket. You'll also need a Nerf football in the bucket and a large bedsheet. Ask two volunteers to hold the bedsheet so that it forms a "net" about six feet off the ground. Explain that one person will stand on one side of the net and toss the item in the bucket over the net. The rest of the group members will stand on the other side of the net and try to catch the object. The person who catches the object gets a point and becomes the next thrower. To demonstrate, pull the Nerf football out of the bucket and toss it over the net. The person who catches it will become the first thrower. Then subtly discard the football and let the thrower discover the actual object he or she will be throwing—the greased fish. Use this activity to lead in to a discussion on being "fooled."

Step 5
Set up a "Folly's Olympics." Schedule "events" to illustrate how frustrating life becomes when normal things are made difficult because of unwise actions. As you describe the events initially, make them seem simple: running through a row of chairs, drawing a picture of a vase of flowers, eating soup, wrapping a package, etc. However, when it's time for kids to actually compete, introduce a "twist" for each event. The people who run through the row of chairs will have their hands and feet tied together. The people who draw a picture of the vase of flowers will be blindfolded. The people who eat soup will have to use a fork. The people who wrap a package will be wearing mittens. Feel free to add your own ideas as well. Afterward, discuss how much more difficult life can be when we don't act wisely.

OPTIONS

SESSION TWO

Step 1
Show some video scenes (which you've screened yourself beforehand) in which the late Peter Sellers plays two very different kinds of "fools." First, show a slapstick scene featuring the bumbling Inspector Clouseau (*A Shot in the Dark*, *Return of the Pink Panther*, *The Pink Panther Strikes Again*, or *Revenge of the Pink Panther*). Then play a segment of *Being There*, in which Sellers portrays the mentally slow gardener, Chance, who knows only what he's seen on TV—but is taken as a genius by the rich and powerful. Afterward, ask: **In what sense is each of these characters a fool? Is one funnier than the other? Why? Are those who think Chance is wise actually fools themselves? Why or why not? How are some people able to "fool" others into thinking they're wise? Can you think of any examples among famous people today?**

Step 5
Play a contemporary Christian song about commitment, such as "Who's on the Lord's Side" by Petra. Discuss how the six types of people described in the session might react to the song. For example, the Mocker might laugh at the idea of being a "fanatic"; the Sluggard might agree that commitment is good, but be too lazy to follow through; the Wise person might be encouraged to consider how committed to Christ he or she really is. Close by asking kids to think about which point of view is closest to their own.

Step 1
Replace Steps 1 and 2 with a shorter opener. Give the group an assignment like rearranging chairs. Then leave the room. What the group won't know is that beforehand you've secretly prepared five kids to play these roles while you're gone: a simpleton (who pretends not to understand and keeps setting up the chairs incorrectly), a fool (who keeps deliberately messing up the chairs), a mocker (who only criticizes what others are doing), a tempter (who tries to lure workers away with refreshments), and a sluggard (who refuses to do anything). After a few minutes, return and discuss what happened.

Step 3
Instead of having everyone skim the Book of Proverbs, have one team study The Wise just as other teams study the other characters. Limit the number of references as follows: The Wise—Proverbs 1:7-10; 10:1, 5, 8, 14; The Simple—9:1-6, 13-18; 14:15, 18; The Fool—12:15, 16; 13:19; 26:11; 28:26; The Mocker—1:22; 21:24; 22:10; The Adulteress—2:16-19; 7:21-23; The Sluggard—6:6-11; 10:26; 21:25. To save more time, combine Steps 4 and 5 as follows. Using a copier that makes enlargements, prepare bigger versions of the cards on Repro Resource 4. (If you can't do that, make signs on poster board.) Post these at intervals around the room. Read the Ten Commandments (Exodus 20:3-17) aloud, one at a time. After each one, have kids stand under the card that they think represents the attitude most kids at school would have toward that commandment. For example, kids might mock one commandment; they might agree with another, but be too lazy to follow it. Let volunteers explain their "stands." To close, have all group members crowd under the "Wise" card and think of one commandment they'll work harder to obey this week.

Step 3
Point out that the end of the Book of Proverbs (31:10-31) gives an insightful description of a wife of noble character. Explain that the passage is written in the form of an acrostic poem, in which each letter of the Hebrew alphabet is used as the first letter of one of the lines of the poem. As a group, create your own acrostic poem about wisdom, using the letters of the alphabet—in order—as the first letters of the lines of the poem. See how many letters you can use. Here's a brief example to get you started:

   Acquiring wisdom should be an everyday goal; it keeps the mind active and brings peace to the soul.
   Believing in God's wisdom will strengthen you daily, when gangs all around you are makin' you crazy.

Step 4
Add the following situation to your discussion of Repro Resource 4:
Situation 4—A fight breaks out in school. You saw the whole thing happen, so you know who started it and what happened.
• **Would you try to break up the fight?**
• **If so, how would you do it? If not, what *would* you do?**
• **After the fight, when the principal is looking for witnesses to tell what happened, what would you do? Why?**

OPTIONS

SESSION TWO

Step 2
Have your kids form groups. Make sure that each group contains both high schoolers and junior highers. Assign one of the "types" of people listed on Repro Resource 3 (Alexis, Wanda, Samantha, etc.) to each group. Once a group is assigned a "type," instruct each member of the group to describe an experience in his or her life in which he or she acted in a way that the "type" of person assigned to the group might have acted. For example, if a group was assigned "Alexis," group members would need to think of a situation in which they thought of something to do that wasn't right and tried to pressure others into doing it. Encourage the high schoolers in each group to respond first to give junior highers an idea of what you're looking for.

Step 3
As you go through the list of the various "types" of people described in Proverbs, ask (for each "type"): **Would you say this type of person is more likely to be a junior higher or a high schooler? Why?** For instance, some kids may say that "The Simple" are more likely to be junior highers because junior highers are more gullible and naive than high schoolers are. Other kids may say that "The Fools" are more likely to be high schoolers because high schoolers have enough experience and knowledge to know what things are wrong, but do them anyway. Of course, this activity will probably stir up a debate between the two age groups, but it may be interesting to hear whether group members associate themselves or other people with each "type" of person.

Step 1
After agreeing on a definition for "fool," ask: **What kinds of people does the world say are foolish?** Answers will probably vary, and may include things like drug users, Christians, people who turn the other cheek, etc. Have someone read aloud I Corinthians 3:19; 4:8-10. Then ask: **What does the world consider to be the benefits or fruits of wisdom?** (Wealth, power, prestige, honor, fame, status, possessions.) **What does Paul consider to be the fruits of wisdom?** Get responses from several group members.

Step 3
As you go through the "types" of people listed in the session, ask volunteers to describe ways in which they've fallen prey to the snares of the Simple, the Fool, the Mocker, the Adulteress, and the Sluggard. If possible, try to get *specific* answers (instead of responses like "Sometimes I make fun of other kids at school"). To insure that you get specific, honest answers, you may want to have kids write their responses anonymously on slips of paper. Then you could collect the slips and read each one aloud. Afterward, as a group, brainstorm some suggestions for avoiding the snares of each "type" of person in the future.

Date Used:

Approx. Time

Step 1: Fooling Around _____
o Extra Action
o Fellowship & Worship
o Mostly Guys
o Extra Fun
o Media
o Short Meeting Time
o Extra Challenge

Step 2: Fool House _____
o Large Group
o Heard It All Before
o Little Bible Background
o Mostly Girls
o Combined Jr. High/High School

Step 3: Fool Proof _____
o Extra Action
o Small Group
o Large Group
o Short Meeting Time
o Urban
o Combined Jr. High/High School
o Extra Challenge

Step 4: What Kind of Fool Am I? _____
o Mostly Guys
o Urban

Step 5: Beyond Folly _____
o Small Group
o Heard It All Before
o Little Bible Background
o Fellowship & Worship
o Mostly Girls
o Extra Fun
o Media

SESSION 3
Hold Your Tongue!

YOUR GOALS FOR THIS SESSION:
Choose one or more

☐ To help kids see what the Book of Proverbs says about proper speech.

☐ To help kids understand how our words are a reflection of our true "heart condition."

☐ To help kids think about their own speech patterns and name specific ways to apply the Proverbs they have studied.

☐ Other _____

Your Bible Base:

Various Proverbs that deal with the way people should speak to one another

CUSTOM CURRICULUM

STEP 1

You Can Say That Again

(Needed: Copies of Repro Resource 5, pencils, paper)

OPTIONS

As kids arrive, don't let anyone talk. Give each person a pencil and a copy of "Fill in the Blanks" (Repro Resource 5) to complete. As kids are working, you should fill in a copy of the Repro Resource with the correct words that appear below. After kids have made their guesses as to how to complete each proverb, collect and shuffle their sheets—along with the one you filled out.

Then give each group member a blank piece of paper and instruct him or her to number it from 1 to 10. Read off three or four of the more plausible responses to the first saying (including the correct one) and have kids write down which one they think is correct. Then shuffle the papers and read off a few possibilities for the second phrase. Continue until you've gone through all ten phrases.

Then read through the correct answers and see who completed the most phrases correctly originally, who guessed the most correct answers after hearing them read, and who got the most people to vote for their made-up answers. Don't reveal the source of each proverb (listed in parentheses) until later.

Here are the correct answers (in capital letters):

1. An enemy will AGREE, but a friend will ARGUE (Russian proverb).
2. When WORDS are many, SIN is not absent (Proverbs 10:19).
3. Don't judge a man by the words of his MOTHER, listen to the comments of his NEIGHBORS (Yiddish proverb).
4. RECKLESS words pierce like a sword, but the TONGUE of the wise brings healing (Proverbs 12:18).
5. Many a man's TONGUE has BROKEN his NOSE (Anonymous).
6. An ANXIOUS heart weighs a man down, but a KIND WORD cheers him up (Proverbs 12:25).
7. Words have WINGS and cannot be RECALLED (Anonymous).
8. A wise man's HEART guides his MOUTH (Proverbs 16:23).
9. SPEECH is the mirror of the SOUL. As a man SPEAKS, so he is (Publius Syrus).
10. A GOSSIP separates close FRIENDS (Proverbs 16:28).

Hand the Repro Resources back to their rightful owners. Then ask: **What do all of these proverbs have in common?** (They all deal with some aspect of people's speech.)

If you had to choose just one of these sayings to memorize, which would you choose, and why? Let kids share their favorite ones, or ones that have special meaning to them. Ask for some specific examples of how some of these proverbs are true.

How many of these sayings would you say are from the Bible? Have kids circle the numbers of the sayings they think are from the Bible. Then have kids indicate their answers with a show of fingers. Congratulate all those who held up five fingers. Ask them to identify which of the sayings are from the Bible. All of the even-numbered ones are from the Book of Proverbs. The others may be true, but they aren't from the Bible.

STEP 2

Word Power

(Needed: Bibles, chalkboard and chalk or newsprint and marker)

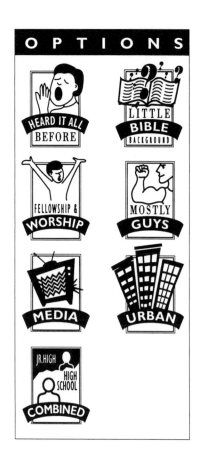

Ask: **How many of you have heard the saying, "Sticks and stones may break my bones but names will never hurt me"?** Ask for a show of hands.

Have you ever used this statement before? If so, under what circumstances? If not, when might someone use it? (The saying is usually used by children who are trying to prove to other children that being teased or called a name doesn't hurt.)

Do you think the saying is true? Why or why not? (While it's true that words probably won't cause physical harm, they can be very painful.)

Assign the following verses to various group members: Proverbs 11:9; Proverbs 12:18; Proverbs 16:24; and Proverbs 18:21. Have them read the verses in succession.

Then ask: **What can we conclude from these verses? Are words good or bad?** (The key thing to see from these verses is that words are very powerful—for good or for bad.)

Say: **Let's make two lists to show the types of words that can hurt or heal.** Draw two columns on the board. Label one "Hurt" and the other "Help."

Then say: **Give me some examples of the types of words—not the words themselves—that can really hurt.** Group members may suggest things like gossip, insults, coarse joking, teasing, lies, etc. List these on the board as they are named.

Ask: **Can the truth ever cause harm?** (Possibly, if it's told in such a way as to purposely upset someone, or if it's told insensitively.)

Give me an example of a time when you were really hurt by something someone said. Let a few kids share. Be prepared to share an example of your own first.

Now give me some examples of the types of words that can help or heal. Group members may suggest things like apologies, compliments, words of encouragement, etc. List these on the board as they are named.

Then say: **Give me an example of a time when someone's words really made you feel better.** Let a few kids share. Again, be prepared to share an example of your own first.

If you put all of the hurtful words you hear in a week on one side of a scale and all of the helpful words you hear in a week on the other side, which side would weigh more? You might want to physically demonstrate this by having kids move to one side of the room or the other to symbolize their answer.

To those who feel they hear more hurtful things in a given week, ask: **Why do you think so many people use hurtful words? How do you respond when someone says something hurtful to you?** Get a few responses.

To those who feel they hear more helpful words in a given week, ask: **Who are you most likely to hear positive words from?** Get a few responses.

Then say: **Let's think about a scale again. But this time, weigh all of the words *you* spoke last week. Which side would weigh more: the hurtful words or the helpful words?** Let kids move around if you choose to have them demonstrate their answers this way.

Then ask: **When are you most likely to use hurtful words?** Get a few responses.

If somebody invented a pill people could take every morning that would cause them to speak only helpful words to one another, would you want to take it? Why or why not? How would your life be different if everybody took this pill? How would your life be different if only you took this pill? Let kids speculate.

Point out that such a pill doesn't exist, but that the Bible is full of "good medicine" concerning how we should speak. Even if other people don't take the Bible's medicine, that's no reason we shouldn't.

STEP 3

Speaking of Proverbs

(Needed: Bibles, copies of Repro Resources 6, copies of Repro Resource 7, pencils, chalkboard and chalk or newsprint and marker)

Say: **I've got good news and bad news. First, the bad news: The Book of Proverbs doesn't ever tell us *what* to say, so we're on our own when it comes to choosing our words. But here's the good news: The Book of Proverbs has a lot to say about *how* we should say things. So while it won't put words in our mouth, it will give us some guiding principles for how we should speak.**

Hand out copies of "The Proverbial List of Proverbs to Paraphrase" (Repro Resource 6). This sheet contains eighteen short passages for kids to look up and paraphrase. If you have a lot of time (yeah, right), let kids work individually, in pairs, or in small groups to paraphrase all eighteen proverbs. Otherwise, divide the passages evenly among individuals, pairs, or small groups, making sure that someone is paraphrasing each passage.

When kids are done paraphrasing, hand out copies of "I Don't Wanna Be Like Mike" (Repro Resource 7). This sheet will give kids a chance to demonstrate how well they understand the verses.

Read (or have kids act out) the first conversation (between Mike and his dad). Then have group members answer these four questions:

1. What is Mike's basic problem in this situation?

2. Which of the verses you just looked up might apply to this situation? Note that some of the verses might apply to more than one situation on Repro Resource 7. For example, Proverbs 16:23 applies to all four.

3. How might these verses help Mike if he were to apply them in the future?

4. What words would have been more appropriate for Mike to use in his response?

Follow the same procedure for each conversation on Repro Resource 7. Use the following to aid your preparation and discussion. Keep in mind, however, that this is just one way of looking at each conversation. See what your kids come up with before sharing anything here.

Conversation #1 (Mike and Dad)

1. Mike's basic problem is that he's lying. He's also trying to use flattery to distract his dad from the real issue.

2. Verses that might apply include Proverbs 14:5; 16:13; 24:26; 26:23-28.

3. These verses all talk about the value of honesty. [NOTE: You don't need to convince your kids that "honesty is the best policy"; instead, ask them why it's sometimes hard to be totally honest.]

4. Obviously, Mike should have said where he really was. [NOTE: In case any of your group members wonder, Mike was watching a movie that his folks told him not to see.]

Conversation #2 (Mike and Mom)

1. Mike's basic problem is that he assumes the worst before he knows what his folks want to talk about. Instead of being calm, he jumps to the wrong conclusion.

2. Verses that might apply include Proverbs 12:16; 15:1; 17:27; 18:13; 25:15.

3. These verses talk about the value of using restraint before speaking. They also talk about the value of speaking gently and without anger.

4. Mike could have avoided a lot of grief if he had said something like, "Sure, what did you want to talk about?" [NOTE: Incidentally, Mike's parents had just read a review of a movie Mike wanted to see, had a change of heart, and wanted to let him know that it's OK for him to see it.]

Conversation #3 (Mike and Mandy)

1. Mike's basic problem is that he keeps saying the wrong things. He isn't choosing his words very carefully.

2. Verses that might apply include Proverbs 10:20, 32; 15:23; 25:11.

3. These verses talk about the value of choosing our words carefully, treating them like choice silver or gold. If Mike had thought a little more about using fitting words, he probably wouldn't have come off as being so offensive.

4. Maybe he shouldn't have commented on the outfit at all, unless he really liked it. If so, he could have said something like, "You look good in that" or "That's a cool outfit. Is it new?"

Conversation #4 (Mike and Mrs. Applegate)

1. Mike's basic problem is that he says too much (not to mention the fact that he's being a sluggard—but that's another session).

2. Verses that might apply include Proverbs 10:19; 11:12; 13:3; 17:28.

3. These verses talk about the value of few words. Mike only makes things worse by going on and on about the teacher's rule. He also gets a jab in at the teacher, which certainly won't help things.

4. Maybe Mike shouldn't have said anything at all. If he felt compelled to say something, he probably should have apologized for not having the paper done on time.

Ask: **Which of the four conversations do you relate to most? Why?** Get a few responses.

You can summarize what Proverbs says about *how* we should speak by writing the following on the board:

Our words should be
- Honest
- Calm
- Apt (or carefully chosen)
- Few

Say: **Our words are more likely to be honest, calm, apt (or carefully chosen), and few if we take some time to weigh them carefully before speaking. I'm sure you've all heard this before, but if you think before speaking, you'll save yourself a lot of grief. But what does it mean to think before speaking? How do we do that?**

The Heart of the Matter

(Needed: Paper, pencils)

Read Proverbs 16:23 together. See how kids paraphrased it earlier. Then explain: **This is a key verse because it tells us that if our heart is in the right place, our words will be too. Instead of focusing on our words, we should focus on our hearts to see if they are right with God. If something's out of whack on the inside, then it only stands to reason that our words will often be inappropriate too.**

I'm going to give you a little "heart test" that you can complete privately. Have kids use the back of one of the Repro Resources to write their responses. **Number your papers from 1 to 10. Answer each question with one of the following responses: "A lot," "Sometimes," "Seldom," or "Never."**

1. How often do you repeat a juicy rumor you've heard about someone else?

2. How often do you swear or make off-color remarks?

3. How often do you put someone down in order to make yourself feel better?

4. How often do you twist the truth in order to avoid negative consequences?

5. How often do you respond to someone without really listening to what the person is saying?

6. How often do you flatter someone without really meaning what you say?

7. How often do you say something about another person behind his or her back that you wouldn't say to his or her face?

8. How often do you betray a friend's confidence?

9. How often do you speak out of anger rather than out of love?

10. How often do you think about stuff like this at church, but then forget about it as soon as you leave?

After kids have written their responses, say: **If you answered "A lot" or "Sometimes" to any of these questions, then you might want to ask God to point out ways you can improve in these areas. If you answered "Never" to every question, then either you're not being honest or you should be leading this session, because you're a lot further along than I am!**

Hold Your Tongue

(Needed: Bibles)

To close the session, have each group member choose one thing he or she will do this week in response to what you've talked about today. Some kids might make a commitment to do something about one area of his or her speech habits. Others might choose a relevant proverb to memorize or apply. Give kids a moment to think of what they want to say.

Add a twist to the activity before kids actually share. Have them "hold their tongues" as they talk. Explain that this exercise should remind them to always think before speaking. For the sake of fairness, you should go first. If your group is large, have kids form teams of four to six to share together.

As you close in prayer, you might want to read aloud Psalm 139:23, 24 and/or Psalm 19:14, asking God to search us and point out to us ways in which our words can be more pleasing to Him.

S T R E E T W I S E

FILL IN THE BLANKS

Complete each saying with words that you think make the most sense. Either try to guess what each proverb actually says, or make up something that might fool someone else into thinking it's the real saying.

1. An enemy will _____, but a friend will _____.

2. When _____ are many, _____ is not absent.

3. Don't judge a man by the words of his _____, listen to the comments of his _____.

4. _____ words pierce like a sword, but the _____ of the wise brings healing.

5. Many a man's _____ has _____ his _____.
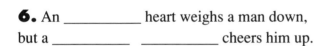

6. An _____ heart weighs a man down, but a _____ _____ cheers him up.

7. Words have _____ and cannot be _____.

8. A wise man's _____ guides his _____.

9. _____ is the mirror of the _____. As a man _____, so he is.

10. A _____ separates close _____.
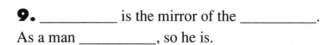

The Proverbial List of Proverbs to Paraphrase

STREETWISE — REPRO RESOURCE 6

Please paraphrase these particular proverbs. In other words, put them into your own words.

Proverbs 10:19

Proverbs 10:20

Proverbs 10:32

Proverbs 11:12

Proverbs 12:16

Proverbs 13:3

Proverbs 14:5

Proverbs 15:1

Proverbs 15:23

Proverbs 16:13

Proverbs 16:23

Proverbs 17:27

Proverbs 17:28

Proverbs 18:13

Proverbs 24:26

Proverbs 25:11

Proverbs 25:15

Proverbs 26:23-28

S T R E E T W I S E

REPRO RESOURCE 7

I DON'T WANNA BE LIKE MIKE

Write down some Proverbs (chapter and verse) from "The Proverbial List of Proverbs to Paraphrase" that Mike should take to heart in each situation.

Proverbs to Apply

Conversation #1
DAD: Where have you been?
MIKE: I was studying at Tom's house.
DAD: Is that so? Tom's mom just called, wondering if Tom's been over here. Do I detect a lie?
MIKE: Dad, you are so clever. Nothing gets past you. I hope that someday I'll be just as good a dad as you. Well, I've gotta run.
DAD: I don't know where you have to run—because you're grounded.

Conversation #2
MOM: Mike, your father and I would like a word with you.
MIKE: What did I do now? I can't believe you guys. Here I am just minding my own business, and you get on my case. I can't believe how suspicious you guys are. When are you going to start trusting me and treat me like an adult?
MOM: Boy, are you edgy. Maybe this isn't a good time to tell you what we wanted to say.

Conversation #3
MANDY: Hi, Mike.
MIKE: Hey, Mandy. Say, is that a new outfit? It's really interesting.
MANDY: What's that supposed to mean?
MIKE: I mean it's unique—one of a kind.
MANDY: Are you saying it's weird?
MIKE: No, I just admire your courage for wearing it.
MANDY: I've gotta go.
MIKE: Where?
MANDY: Home to change.

Conversation #4
MRS. APPLEGATE: Turn in your papers before you leave. If yours isn't finished, turn it in Monday. I'll dock you one letter grade for each day it's late.
MIKE: I had every intention of finishing the paper, but something came up that was completely beyond my control and I didn't get it done. I think it's unfair to dock me when you don't even know the circumstances that resulted in its being late. You're not even taking into account the fact that I turned in two of the last three papers on time. Besides, you didn't say you'd lower our grade if it was late, so I don't see how you can make up new rules as we go along here. I wish you'd be a little more considerate of our needs for a change.
MRS. APPLEGATE: Someday you'll thank me for this. See you Monday, Mike.

OPTIONS

S E S S I O N   T H R E E

Step 1

Instead of using Repro Resource 5, play "Weighing Your Words." Collect twenty-six flat, smooth stones or blocks in widely varying sizes and weights. On the front and back of each object write a letter of the alphabet—with different letters on the front and back of any one object. Put the objects in a box. Bring them, along with a bathroom scale, to the meeting. Have kids form two teams. The first team will dump the objects on the floor and, in one minute, try to form the *heaviest* word it can, using the letters that are showing on the objects. Using the scale, weigh the word the team comes up with. Then give the other team a chance. Play as many rounds as you have time for. The team with the most verbal poundage at the end of the game wins. Use this as an introduction to the idea of weighing our words—being careful about what we say.

Step 3

Have two volunteers practice the conversations from Repro Resource 7. Meanwhile, divide the Repro Resource 6 verses among the rest of the group. Give each person (other than the two actors) a marker and a sheet of poster board for each verse he or she has. Each person should write his or her paraphrase on the poster board. As the first conversation is acted out, each person with a verse that applies should run behind the actors and hold up the sign so the group can see it. Have your actors replay the conversation until all applicable verses have been shown. After discussing briefly how the verses apply, repeat the process with the other conversations.

Step 1

Instead of having kids work on Repro Resource 5 individually, work on it together as a group. And instead of filling out the sheet according the instructions, use it for a "Madlibs" game. You will ask group members to supply you with words, giving them only the part of speech you're looking for (noun, verb, adjective, etc.). The first word kids call out for each blank is the word you will write down. The parts of speech you'll look for to fill in Repro Resource 5 are as follows: (1) verb, verb; (2) plural noun, noun; (3) noun, noun; (4) adjective, noun; (5) noun, past-tense verb, noun; (6) adjective, adjective, noun; (7) noun, past-tense verb; (8) noun, noun; (9) noun, noun, plural verb; (10) noun, plural noun. After you've filled in all of the blanks, read back what group members have come up with. (Chances are you'll get sentences like "Many a man's turtle has punched his shoelaces.") Then read and discuss the correct proverbs.

Step 5

As you wrap up the session, try a memorization activity to help kids remember some of the relevant information from the session. On the board, write the references for several of the proverbs you studied in this session (Proverbs 10:19; 11:9; 12:18, 25; 16:23, 24, 28; 18:21). See how many of the verses group members can memorize together. Then, rather than having the group recite the verses in unison, have members recite the verses one word at a time—with kids taking turns saying each word. You might want to award a prize for each verse the group successfully recites.

Step 1

After you go through Repro Resource 5, have kids form groups of four to six. Instruct each group to come up with its own proverb about the "tongue" or being careful of what we say. You might want to reread a couple of the proverbs from Repro Resource 5 to give the groups an idea of what you're looking for. Encourage group members to come up with short proverbs that are witty, clever, and/or humorous. The proverbs should also apply to the lives of kids today. After a few minutes, have a spokesperson from each group stand and recite his or her group's proverb. Then have group members vote on which proverb was best. Award prizes (perhaps tongue depressors) to the winning group.

Step 3

Have kids form groups of six. Assign each group one of the situations on Repro Resource 7. Explain that two members of the group will act out the assigned situation. The other four members will then each answer one of the questions from the session regarding the situation ("What is Mike's problem in this situation?" "Which of the verses [from Repro Resource 6] might apply to this situation?" "How might these verses help Mike if he were to apply them in the future?" "What words would have been more appropriate for Mike to use in his response?"). Give the groups a few minutes to work. When everyone is finished, have each group present its situation and responses.

OPTIONS

SESSION THREE

Heard It All Before

Step 2
Kids may resist the idea of being careful about words, thinking that so much self-control will take the fun out of life. Use the following questions to introduce the idea of thinking before speaking. Have kids answer with the first reply that comes to mind. (1) **Is the Pledge of Allegiance sung more often at baseball games or football games?** (It isn't sung at all.) (2) **Do more people go to lunch at 11:30 a.m. or 12 a.m.?** (11:30; 12 a.m. is midnight.) (3) **In what country did the wall between North and South Berlin fall?** (None; the wall was between East and West Berlin.) (4) **Who was President of the U.S. when Sherlock Holmes was alive?** (Sherlock Holmes was never alive; he was fictional.) (5) **If S is the symbol for the element known as sulfur, what is the symbol for the element known as salt?** (Salt is a compound, not an element.) Point out that just as blurting out an "obvious" answer may cause us to flunk a quiz, blurting out the first angry or sarcastic words we think of can wreck relationships. Weighing our words can protect us as well as others.

Step 3
Skip the "good news, bad news" paragraph. Your kids probably don't *want* anyone to tell them what to say; they want freedom to express themselves. Since most of the session's emphasis is on what *not* to say, take a breather and affirm the freedom God gives us to say things in our own individual styles. Encourage kids to be as creative as possible in their Proverbs paraphrases and in their suggestions for what Mike should have said. In Step 5, have kids compete to see who can come up with the most creative way to communicate the sentiments of "Have a nice day" or "May the road rise to meet you; may the wind be always at your back" in their own words.

Little Bible Background

Step 2
Rather than having your kids look up the verses from Proverbs and try to interpret what they're saying, try another activity. Have your kids form teams. Instruct each team to think of as many fictional stories and real-life situations as possible in which words have a powerful effect. For instance, God created the universe by speaking it into existence. A state governor can stop an execution by granting a pardon to the condemned person. In the movie *The Day the Earth Stood Still*, the heroine must say certain words to prevent the world from being destroyed. After a few minutes, have each team share its list. Use this activity to lead in to the discussion on which types of words are good and which are bad.

Step 3
Kids with little Bible background may have difficulty paraphrasing the passages on Repro Resource 6 by themselves or in a small group. So choose eight of the passages to work on as a group. (The following passages apply best to Repro Resource 7, so you might want to consider using them: Proverbs 10:19; 10:32; 12:16; 15:1; 15:23; 16:13; 17:28; 26:23-28.) Read each passage aloud. Then ask three group members to explain (in their own words) what they think it means. After all three have shared, have the rest of the group vote on which explanation makes the most sense—or suggest ways to combine the three definitions to create a new one. Write each passage and its agreed-upon paraphrase on the board for use later in the session.

Fellowship & Worship

Step 2
After pointing out that "Sticks and stones may break my bones but names will never hurt me" is not necessarily true, focus on the flip side of the statement. Explain that if words have the power to hurt, they also have the power to encourage. Organize a brief "complimentfest" in which group members mingle around, giving "pick me up" compliments to each other. Emphasize that the compliments don't have to be "major" ("You're the smartest girl I've ever known"). Instead, they should focus on "minor," everyday things ("That joke you made last week about Daniel in the lions' den was really funny"; "I saw you playing basketball after school yesterday; you've got a good jump shot"). Afterward, have volunteers share some other examples of when words made them feel better.

Step 5
As you wrap up the session, lead your group members in singing a couple of hymns that deal with the "tongue" or the words that come from our mouths. Among the hymns you might consider are "O for a Thousand Tongues to Sing" and "Take My Life" (focusing on the second verse: "Take my voice and let it sing . . .").

OPTIONS

SESSION THREE

MOSTLY GIRLS

MOSTLY GUYS

EXTRA FUN

Mostly Girls

Step 3
Ask: **How many of you know what the "ten-second rule" is?** If your girls don't know, encourage them to make up a plausible-sounding possibility. Then explain that the ten-second rule applies to how we speak. Before we say something that maybe we shouldn't, we should count to ten and decide what effect our words might have. Give your group members a chance to practice this. One at a time, have each girl come to the front of the room, close her eyes, and count to ten. When she opens her eyes, she should describe everything she sees in a positive, nice, non-cutting way. (For instance, she may comment on the ugly—or, rather, "practical"—wallpaper.) Give each of your group members a chance to "practice."

Step 4
Have your group members sit in a circle. Write on a piece of paper, "Did you hear about Matilda? I heard she got caught _____." [NOTE: If you have a girl named Matilda in your group or know of a girl named Matilda in the area, use another name.] Pass the paper and pencil to the person on your right. Give her fifteen seconds to add to the rumor or create a new one involving Matilda. Then have her pass the paper to the person on her right, who will continue the process. Encourage the girls to keep their rumors lighthearted and humorous. When the paper comes around to you again, read aloud the rumors your girls came up with. Afterward, ask: **Do you think girls are more likely to gossip than guys are? Explain. What are some situations in which gossip typically occurs? How can a person stop gossip before it occurs?** Encourage most of your group members to respond to these questions.

Mostly Guys

Step 1
Point out that although there are a lot of ways that the tongue can do damage—through unclean talking or joking, backbiting, cutting down others, etc.—it can also be very helpful to others and to us. To demonstrate this, have your guys compete in a bubble gum bubble-blowing contest. Give each of your guys a piece of gum. Allow one minute for the contestants to chew the gum and get it into prime bubble-blowing shape. Then call the contestants to the front of the room one at a time and give them thirty seconds to blow a bubble as big as possible. You will serve as judge for the event. After everyone has had an opportunity to blow a bubble, declare a winner and give him a pack of gum as a prize.

Step 2
Say: **"Sticks and stones may break my bones, but names will never hurt me." How many of you believe that's true?** Probably many of your guys will raise their hands or indicate that they think it's true. Chances are that name-calling *does* affect them as much as it does anyone else; however, they're afraid to admit that they can be hurt by "simple words." If several of your guys raise their hands, say: **Wow, you guys must be pillars of strength. When I was your age, I remember that names hurt a lot.** If possible, share an experience from your youth in which you were hurt by being called a name. Then discuss why guys try to pretend that they're unaffected by names.

Extra Fun

Step 1
Have kids form teams. Give each team three pieces of poster board, several colored markers, and a sheet of paper on which you've written three proverbs or short sayings. Among the proverbs/sayings you might use are "The early bird gets the worm"; "Early to bed, early to rise makes a man healthy, wealthy, and wise"; "A stitch in time saves nine"; etc. Instruct the teams to illustrate each of their assigned proverbs/sayings on the individual sheets of poster board. For instance, one team might draw a bird—wearing a watch that reads "4:30 a.m."—pulling a worm out of a hole (to illustrate "The early bird gets the worm"). After a few minutes, have each team display its posters while the rest of the group tries to guess what proverbs/sayings are being illustrated.

Step 5
As you wrap up the session, organize a game to illustrate that our mouths can (and should) be used positively. Have kids form two teams (dividing up guys and girls evenly on each team). Instruct each team to line up guy-girl-guy-girl for the old "pass-the-Lifesaver-on-a-toothpick" contest. Distribute toothpicks and instruct kids to put them in their mouth. Then give the first person in each line a Lifesaver candy. When you say, Go, he or she will put the Lifesaver on his or her toothpick and then "transfer" the candy (without using his or her hands) to the toothpick of the next person in line. If, during a transfer, the Lifesaver falls to the ground, the team must start over with a new piece of candy. The first team to successfully pass its Lifesaver to the end of the line wins. You might want to award prizes to the winning team.

OPTIONS

SESSION THREE

MEDIA

Step 2
During the week, videotape about twenty seconds of a positive, warmhearted children's TV character (Barney the Dinosaur or Mister Rogers, for example) talking. Then videotape about twenty seconds of a sarcastic TV character (like Murphy Brown or Bud Bundy [*Married with Children*]) putting someone down. Follow this with twenty more seconds of a kindly children's TV character, then twenty more seconds of a sarcastic one. At this point in the session, play the whole tape. Contrast the helpful and hurting words and their effect. Ask: **Are children the only ones who need to be built up instead of put down? Why do you suppose so much comedy today is based on criticizing people? If everyone gave up putting people down, would we all have to talk like** [name of kindly children's TV character you showed]**? Why or why not?**

Step 3
In place of Conversation #4 on Repro Resource 7, play one or two secular rap songs on tape or CD (after first listening to them yourself). Ask: **Which verses might apply here? Are the words honest? Calm? Carefully chosen? Few?** (Some rap songs [and songs in other styles] tend to be the opposite—boastful, agitated, reckless, and repetitive.) Point out that some rap music gets away with making statements that some listeners might like to make, but can't. Ask: **What do you think the author(s) of Proverbs would say about people who are careful with their words but enjoy listening to musicians, actors, and comedians who aren't?**

SHORT MEETING TIME

Step 1
Replace Steps 1 and 2 with the following opener. Have kids stand in a circle, facing outward, so that no one can see anyone else's back. Tape to each person's back a sign that reads "OK." But say: **I'm taping a sign to your back. Yours says either "OK" or "Weird."** Then have everyone turn to look at the back of one group member, who doesn't get to turn around. Kids shouldn't say what the person's sign says, but can say "Oh" or "Hmm." Do the same with another group member, and then another. Afterward, ask kids how they felt. Talk about the power of words—how they can hurt. Then let kids remove their signs and see that they're all "OK." Talk about the power of words to help. Ask: **Do you hear more hurtful or helpful words in a week? Why? How does that affect you?** Then go to the end of Step 2, asking the questions about the hypothetical pill that could cause everyone to say only helpful words.

Step 3
Skip Repro Resource 6. Instead, have kids form three teams. Assign Team A the first conversation from Repro Resource 7 and these references: Proverbs 14:5; 16:13; 24:26; 26:23-28. Assign Team B the second conversation and these references: Proverbs 12:16; 15:1; 17:27; 18:13; 25:15. Assign Team C the third conversation and these references: Proverbs 10:20, 32; 15:23; 25:11. Skip the fourth conversation and its references. Instruct each team to look up its assigned verses, act out its conversation for the rest of the group, and explain how the verses relate. Skip Step 5. Close in silent prayer, letting kids talk to God about the way they talk.

URBAN

Step 2
The saying "Sticks and stones may break my bones, but names will never hurt me" hits close to home with urban kids, who probably face the threat of "sticks and stones" (violence) more often than most other kids. So for an urban youngster, being called a name actually may be the lesser of two evils—when you consider the alternative. But still, names can hurt. Have kids form small groups. Instruct the members of each group to come up with a list of names and insults that they hear every day at school or on the street. Ask them to focus on words or insults that are used specifically by urban young people. (They should *not*, however, list any expletives or vulgarities.) After a few minutes, have each group share its list. Then discuss which names and insults seem especially hurtful and which seem (relatively) "harmless." Ask kids to explain their reasoning.

Step 3
Give your urban teens an opportunity to paraphrase, using hip-hop slang, some of the proverbs listed on Repro Resource 6. Have kids form groups of three or four. Assign each group one (or more) of the proverbs on the sheet. Instruct each group to read its assigned passage and then restate it, using words and phrases that they're comfortable with. After a few minutes, have each group share its paraphrase. Afterward, have kids vote by applause on which paraphrase was the "hippest-hoppest" version. Here's an example from Proverbs 10:19: "Too much talkin' means sin is somewhere frontin', but those who cap their lip are b-b-bumpin' on the wise tip."

OPTIONS

SESSION THREE

Step 2
Have your junior highers and high schoolers make a list of as many put-downs and cutting remarks as they can think of that they've heard in school lately. (Keep them clean.) After a few minutes, have each person share his or her list. Write the put-downs and remarks on the board as kids share them, making a high school list and a junior high list. After all of the group members have shared, compare the high schoolers' list with the junior highers'. Do you notice any trends among each age group? Are one group's remarks more vicious and cutting than the other's? If so, why do your kids suppose that is? After you've discussed the differences between the two lists, go through each remark on the lists, asking your group members how the person to whom the remark was directed may have felt about it.

Step 5
It would be nice to end this session with a time of affirmation in which group members use their words to compliment and encourage each other. Unfortunately, in a mixed group, your kids may be hesitant to do much face-to-face complimenting. (High schoolers especially may feel uncomfortable about being "extra nice" to junior highers.) So give your kids an opportunity to share "anonymous" compliments. You'll need several valentines (the kind little kids exchange at school). Make sure the valentines are friendship-oriented, and do not include romantic sentiments. Distribute the valentines. Instruct each person to prepare a valentine for every other group member, writing a heartfelt compliment for the person who will receive it. After a few minutes, collect the valentines and then distribute them to the appropriate people.

Step 1
Once your group members have completed the proverbs on Repro Resource 5, spend some time discussing why each proverb is true and brainstorming some situations in which the truth of each proverb is proved. For instance, for #1, you might ask: **Aren't friends supposed to agree with us and enemies disagree?** (Not necessarily. If a person is wrong about something, his or her enemies won't care. The person's friends, however, *will* care, and will seek to correct him or her—even if it means arguing with him or her.) **Name a situation in which an enemy would agree with someone and a friend would argue.** As time allows, go through all ten proverbs.

Step 4
After going through the ten questions in the session, have your group members each create a "code of ethics" for their speech habits (based on the questions themselves and the proverbs you covered in the session). Explain that the code should be as specific as possible ("I will not . . ." "When I hear other people violating this code, I will . . ."). After a few minutes, have volunteers read their codes to the rest of the group. Then encourage kids to keep their codes in a place where they'll see them often in the coming week. Have them keep track of how well they follow their codes and report back next week.

Date Used:

Approx. Time

Step 1: You Can Say That Again _____
o Extra Action
o Small Group
o Large Group
o Mostly Guys
o Extra Fun
o Short Meeting Time
o Extra Challenge

Step 2: Word Power _____
o Heard It All Before
o Little Bible Background
o Fellowship & Worship
o Mostly Guys
o Media
o Urban
o Combined Jr. High/High School

Step 3: Speaking of Proverbs _____
o Extra Action
o Large Group
o Heard It All Before
o Little Bible Background
o Mostly Girls
o Media
o Short Meeting Time
o Urban

Step 4: The Heart of the Matter _____
o Mostly Girls
o Extra Challenge

Step 5: Hold Your Tongue _____
o Small Group
o Fellowship & Worship
o Extra Fun
o Combined Jr. High/High School

SESSION 4
The Meaning of Life

YOUR GOALS FOR THIS SESSION:
Choose one or more

☐ To help kids get a basic grasp of the main themes of Ecclesiastes.

☐ To help kids understand how meaningless life is apart from God.

☐ To help kids evaluate how meaningful various things are to them and concentrate more on areas that really matter.

☐ Other _____

Your Bible Base:

Selected portions of Ecclesiastes

Is There a Flaw in Murphy's Law?

(Needed: Copies of Repro Resource 8, pencils)

Arrange to have something go wrong just as your session is about to begin. Maybe the electricity could go off, or you could "lose" your teaching materials, or another group could come and demand use of your room—anything out of the ordinary. After dealing with your temporary crisis, explain that it is a good example of "Murphy's Law."

Ask: **How many of you have heard of Murphy's Law? If so, what is it?** (Murphy's Law states that "If anything can go wrong, it will.") As group members respond, hand out copies of "Murphy's Law" (Repro Resource 8) and pencils.

Say: **Give me some examples of how you've seen Murphy's Law at work lately.** Get a few responses.

As you look over these other "laws," which ones can you relate to? Why? Let kids share for a while.

At the bottom of the sheet there's a place for you to coin your own version of Murphy's Law. Let's see what you can come up with. Give kids a minute or two to come up with some type of law or rule and a title for it. The first word in the title should be the person's name—last or first—and the second should be some other word like law, observation, theory, hypothesis, etc. Have some volunteers share their ideas.

Then ask: **What do all of these statements have in common?** (They all are from a negative or pessimistic view of life.)

How many of them would you say are true all of the time? Kids will probably point out that most of these statements are true sometimes, but not all of the time. It may *seem* like they are true all of the time, but that doesn't mean they are.

Do any of the "laws" on the sheet sound familiar? If so, where have you heard or seen them before? See if your group members recognize that several of the laws are from the Bible. Can they guess which ones? It's not too hard to figure out, but we've made it easy for you to tell. All of the ones starting with the letters A through F are from the Book of Ecclesiastes. Explain that you'll be looking more closely at Ecclesiastes today. Point out that upon first reading, some people think the book is depressing.

Say: **Today we're going to see why such a "pessimistic" book is included in the Bible.**

STEP 2

A Real Downer

(Needed: Bibles, paper, pencils, chalkboard and chalk or newsprint and marker)

Since Ecclesiastes is probably unfamiliar territory to most of your group, it would be ideal to read the whole book together. If that's not possible, assign kids to read aloud the following sections (in order):
- Ecclesiastes 1:1-11
- Ecclesiastes 1:12-18
- Ecclesiastes 2:1-11
- Ecclesiastes 2:15-23
- Ecclesiastes 4:1-4
- Ecclesiastes 4:7, 8
- Ecclesiastes 5:10-17
- Ecclesiastes 6:1-9
- Ecclesiastes 6:10-12
- Ecclesiastes 8:14-17
- Ecclesiastes 9:3-6
- Ecclesiastes 9:11, 12
- Ecclesiastes 11:8-10
- Ecclesiastes 12:1, 6-8
- Ecclesiastes 12:9-14

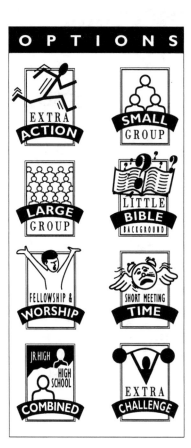

Ask group members to read the passages in their most depressing, "woe-is-me" voices. Instruct those who are listening to write down any key words or phrases they hear multiple times.

Afterward, ask: **How do you feel after hearing these verses?** Point out that the passages are not very uplifting. In fact, some say they're downright depressing. If your group members read only the passages listed previously, then they skipped over some of the more positive sections like Ecclesiastes 3:1-22 and 4:9-12.

From what we read, who do you think wrote these words? Have kids review Ecclesiastes 1:1, 12-16; 2:4-9; 12:9. These verses all suggest that the author is King Solomon. However, it's also possible that someone wrote it at a later date as if it were Solomon speaking.

Assuming Solomon wrote these words, how does it make you feel to know that one of the wisest and richest people who ever lived felt this way? If no one mentions it, point out that how rich, good-looking, or smart we are is no guarantee of our happiness.

Why do you think such depressing words are contained in the Bible? The answer to this question will become clearer after taking a closer look at some of the phrases that are repeated. So allow group members to offer their opinions, but hold off on answering this question right away.

Of the verses that we just read, were there any that surprised you or that really made you stop and think? If so, what were they?

What are some of the key words or phrases that appear multiple times in these verses? See what kids wrote down as they listened to the verses being read. Also let them look at the passages again and call things out.

Use the following information to supplement group members' responses. The reference in parentheses is the first verse in Ecclesiastes in which the word is mentioned. You might want to write the information on the board as you share it.

• "Meaningless" (1:2)—This word appears well over thirty times in Ecclesiastes.

• "Under the sun" (1:3)—This phrase appears about thirty times in the book.

• "Work," "toil," "labor" (1:3)—These words appear over twenty-five times.

• "God" (1:13)—This word appears almost thirty times.

• "Chasing after the wind" (1:14)—This phrase appears at least nine times.

• "Eat and drink and find satisfaction" (2:24, 25)—Variations of this phrase appear at least six times.

A Meaningless Exercise

(Needed: Bibles)

Say: **Let's take a closer look at some of these phrases to help us better understand the book.**

What are some of the things the writer of Ecclesiastes says are meaningless? Have kids skim the verses and call things out as they find them. Among the answers group members might come up with are "everything" (1:1; 12:8), "all the things that are done under the sun" (1:14), "pleasure" (2:1), achievements (2:11), "being wise" (2:15), "work" (2:17), pain and grief over work (2:23), people who work hard but aren't content with what they have (4:7, 8), loving money (5:10); not being able to enjoy one's wealth and possessions (6:2), a roving appetite (6:9), "righteous men who get what the wicked deserve" and vice versa (8:14), "everything to come" (11:8), and "youth and vigor" (11:10).

Have you ever felt "everything" was meaningless? If so, when? Why did you feel that way? When might someone feel that way today? What would your life be like if you felt everything was totally meaningless? Use questions like these to get kids thinking about what the author of Ecclesiastes might be saying.

Knowing what you know about the rest of the Bible, how would you complete this sentence: "Everything is meaningless when . . ."? Group members may give responses like "Everything is meaningless when you don't have Jesus in your life" or "Everything is meaningless when you try to live your life apart from God" or "Everything is meaningless when you try to do things on your own." You might want to point out that Matthew 16:26 is a great New Testament counterpart to this statement. Matthew 16:26 tells us that nothing is accomplished if a person gains the whole world, but loses his or her soul.

Read a few of the "under the sun" references from Ecclesiastes 1:3, 9, 14; 2:11, 17; 8:17. Then ask: **Where exactly is this place "under the sun"?** If no one mentions it, point out that the phrase is probably referring to earth. Verse 8:17 is the key. God is over and above His creation. We can't comprehend what He has done. So if we keep God out of the picture, things will be meaningless. God isn't confined to a place "under the sun."

What is the phrase "chasing after the wind" referring to? (Any meaningless, futile activity.)

What are some things people do that amount to nothing more than wind chasing? (Acquiring more and more things, only to leave them behind when you die; watching a lot of television shows; etc.)

Read the following passages in quick succession: Ecclesiastes 2:24, 25; 3:12, 13, 22; 5:18-20; 8:15; 9:7.

Then ask: **What are these verses saying?** (The most a person can expect out of life is to eat, drink, and enjoy his or her work. These things are gifts from God.)

Is the writer of Ecclesiastes saying that all there is to life is eating, drinking, and working? (No. He's saying it is a gift from God to be able to enjoy life. Viewing things from this side of the cross, we know how much more God has in store for us. The writer of Ecclesiastes didn't have this same view.)

Is the writer saying it's OK to party all the time? If not, what is he saying? (No. He's saying to enjoy life, not to overindulge ourselves.)

Does Ecclesiastes 12:13 add anything to our understanding

of the book? If no one mentions it, point out that this verse is the summation of the matter: Life lived apart from God (under the sun) is totally meaningless. The only possible conclusion for someone who keeps God out of the picture is despair. But there's another alternative: to live for God. Those who fear God and keep His commandments will find enjoyment in their daily lives, not to mention the afterlife.

Say: **A preacher once said that the Bible is the cradle of Christ and, like the manger, it has some straw in it. This preacher once said that the Book of Ecclesiastes is some of the straw that needs be be thrown out. Given the little we've looked into it today, would you tend to agree or disagree with this statement?** If no one mentions it, suggest that it's very dangerous to start discarding parts of the Bible. Maybe instead of throwing Ecclesiastes out, we should seek to learn what we can from it. Maybe it's there to get us thinking about what life is really all about and how senseless it is without God.

Vanity Plates

(Needed: Copies of Repro Resource 9, pencils)

Hand out copies of "License to Talk" (Repro Resource 9). Let group members work in pairs to complete the sheet. Each license plate represents a type of person who echoes some of the sentiments expressed in Ecclesiastes. Kids are to think about what they would say to each person. After a few minutes, ask volunteers to share their responses. If you have time, ask kids to speculate on what kind of car each license plate might be seen on.

Use the following information to guide your discussion as necessary.

I C I BUY (I see, I buy)
What might this plate tell you about the person who chose it? (The person probably likes to shop and probably has a lot of money—or a large credit card debt.)
What might you say to this person to get a conversation started? What questions could you ask this person to get him or her thinking about what really matters in life? (Why do you like to shop so much? What's the last thing you bought that really brought you lasting happiness?)

Ask: **What's the last thing *you* bought in order to make** yourself happy? How do you feel about that thing now? What's something you really want to buy right now? How much happiness will that thing bring you in ten years?** Get several responses.

I PARTY

What might this plate tell you about the person who chose it? (The person enjoys a good time. Maybe the person enjoys drinking. Maybe the person sells Tupperware.)

What might you say to this person to get a conversation started? What questions could you ask this person to get him or her thinking about what really matters in life? (What's the greatest party you've ever been to? What was so great about it? Are there ever times when you don't feel like partying? If so, when?)

Ask: **Why do you think some kids are really into partying? What's going through their minds before, during, and after the party? What was going through your mind at the last party you went to? Why were you there?** Get several responses.

MAKE LUV

What might this plate tell you about the person who chose it? (The person probably enjoys having sex. Maybe the person advocates a "free love" value system. Maybe the person is a peace activist.)

What might you say to this person to get a conversation started? What questions could you ask this person to get him or her thinking about what really matters in life? (Why did you feel compelled to put that message on your license plate? What does it mean to "make love"? What's the connection between love and sex? Do you think most people find lasting fulfillment in sexual relationships?)

Ask: **Do you think people who are sleeping around are happier than those who aren't? Why or why not? If sex doesn't give people lasting fulfillment, why are so many people having sex outside of marriage?** Get several responses.

ALL WORK

[NOTE: You might want to point out that this person's other car says "NO PLAY."]

What might this plate tell you about the person who chose it? (The person probably feels like he or she works too much. The person is probably working hard to get ahead.)

What might you say to this person to get a conversation started? What questions could you ask this person to get him or her thinking about what really matters in life? (What kind of work do you do? Why do you work so hard? What would happen if you didn't work so hard? Do you enjoy your work?)

Ask: **Why do you think some people are workaholics? Do**

you think you could become a workaholic? Why or why not? How important do you think work is to your parents? Why? Get several responses.

Summarize: **The Book of Ecclesiastes has something to say to all of these people. It was written for anyone who questions what life is all about or who's seeking fulfillment in some way that doesn't involve God. Even in Bible times, people were looking to things like materialism, sex, drinking, and work to find fulfillment in life. The bottom line is that life has no meaning if it's lived apart from God. All of these things might bring temporary pleasure, but in the scope of a lifetime, they mean nothing apart from God. That's what the Book of Ecclesiastes is all about.**

A Lot on Your Plate

(Needed: Bibles, paper, markers, scissors, license plate [optional])

Continue with the vanity-plate idea by having kids create their own vanity plates. These plates should convey some type of positive message about what really matters in life. Give kids a supply of blank paper and markers. If possible, try to use paper that is roughly the same size and shape as an actual license plate. You could even photocopy a real license plate and then white out the letters and numerals. The idea is to have kids make their plates look as real as possible.

Here are a few examples that we came up with. Don't share them unless your kids are having trouble coming up with their own.
GOD IS
HES RISN
JOHN 316
NEW LIFE
I MATTER
ASK ME 1

After a few minutes, ask group members to share their creations.

Then say: **Pretend that you're seventy years old and you're looking back on your life. What things in your life right now will still matter then? What things will seem totally unimportant?** Get a few responses.

Then ask: **How can you get your friends who don't have a**

relationship with Jesus to see that a life lived apart from God is meaningless? Get several responses.

Close the session in prayer, thanking God for bringing real meaning to our lives. Psalm 90 offers many parallels to the Book of Ecclesiastes and may serve as a fitting prayer—especially verse 12.

STREETWISE

REPRO RESOURCE 8

Murphy's Law

Murphy's Law: If anything can go wrong, it will.

Henning's Corollary: Nothing is ever as easy as it looks.

Grocke's Gripe: Everything takes longer than you think.

LeFever's Lesson: Everything goes wrong at once.

Quartermain's Commentary on Murphy's Law: Murphy was an optimist.

Adair's Axiom: Everything is meaningless.

Nagle's Theory: If it ain't broke, it will be soon.

Parker's Principle: If it's raining, it must be the weekend.

Brinkman's Observation: There's nothing new under the sun.

Irwin's Rule: When riding your bike, it's always uphill and against the wind.

Jackson's Finding: If you paid full price, it will go on sale tomorrow.

Cook's Comment: All things are wearisome.

Duckworth's Dilemma: What is twisted cannot be straightened.

Kwon's Creed: The other line always moves faster (unless you switch to it).

Edington's Eulogy: Of making many books there is no end.

Mephibosheth's Message: When called upon to read the Bible out loud, your passage will have a lot of difficult names to pronounce.

Forsyth's Finding: Much study wearies the body.

Ogleby's Lament: All the good ones are already taken.

Develop your own law, corollary, rule, axiom, theorem, observation, principle, or whatever along the lines of Murphy's Law. Give it a fancy title too.

_____ _____:

S T R E E T W I S E

LICENSE TO TALK

REPRO RESOURCE
9

Sometimes vanity plates say a lot about the person who chose them. Here are some actual vanity plates that have been spotted on the highway. Answer the questions for each one.

What might this plate tell you about the person who chose it?

What might you say to this person to get a conversation started? What questions could you ask this person to get him or her thinking about what really matters in life?

What might this plate tell you about the person who chose it?

What might you say to this person to get a conversation started? What questions could you ask this person to get him or her thinking about what really matters in life?

What might this plate tell you about the person who chose it?

What might you say to this person to get a conversation started? What questions could you ask this person to get him or her thinking about what really matters in life?

What might this plate tell you about the person who chose it?

What might you say to this person to get a conversation started? What questions could you ask this person to get him or her thinking about what really matters in life?

OPTIONS

SESSION FOUR

Step 1
Before the session, buy or make a piñata. Don't put any prizes or candy inside. (If you bought one with goodies in it, perform surgery and take them out.) Hang the piñata from the ceiling or a tree. But don't let kids know the piñata's empty. To start the meeting, blindfold the kids and let them take turns trying to smash the piñata with a broom handle. After several minutes, tear the piñata open to reveal that nothing's inside. Tie this into the view that life is a difficult, meaningless attempt to find our way in the dark—with no reward at the end.

Step 2
Have group members line up. Tie each person's arm and leg to the next person's arm and leg, chain-gang style (but with crepe paper or yarn, not chains). Then get the group trudging around the room, singing either "That's the sound of the men working on a chain gang . . ." or the "Yo-ee-oh" chant of the Wicked Witch's castle guards in *The Wizard of Oz*. Kids must keep up, but not go too fast. Anyone who breaks the chain will be re-tied and become leader of the singing or chanting. Kids must carry Bibles. Call out the fifteen Ecclesiastes references; each person must read one in a "woe-is-me" voice. Let several kids read different passages simultaneously to save time.

Step 2
To accentuate the content and mood of the Book of Ecclesiastes, introduce the Bible study in your most depressed, subdued, couldn't-care-less-one-way-or-the-other voice. Say: **Since most of you probably aren't familiar with Ecclesiastes, I guess we might as well read some of it.** (Yawn.) **Well, maybe not. All it talks about is how everything is meaningless, so why even read it? Who really cares?** Stand in a spaced-out, comatose-like state for a few seconds. Then say: **Actually, I guess I probably should read this to you guys, since that's my job. So, if you feel like it, open up your Bibles . . .** Open your Bible slowly, and start lethargically thumbing your way through it—until it just "slips" out of your hand. Stare at it on the floor for a few seconds. Then "snap out of it" and shift back into your normal, excited-youth-worker mode! Ask: **Do you ever feel that way about life sometimes? Kind of like a slug? Asking, "Who really cares?"? The writer of Ecclesiastes describes life as being "meaningless"—if you try to live it without God. Let's see what he says.** Assign group members the passages from Ecclesiastes to read. Then answer the accompanying questions as a group.

Step 3
To introduce the idea of chasing after the wind, stage a quick contest. You'll need a hand-held, battery-operated fan; a box of facial tissues; and a stopwatch. Have kids take turns seeing how long they can keep a tissue afloat, using just the wind power from the fan. Each contestant may move around the room as much as necessary, but may not touch the tissue with any part of his or her body or allow the tissue to touch the floor.

Step 1
If your group is too unwieldy to cover Repro Resource 8 together, try a different opening activity instead. Briefly explain the concept of Murphy's Law and read some of its variations from Repro Resource 8. Then have kids form groups of six. Announce that the members of each group will compete to see who can come up with the most variations of Murphy's Law. Have the members of each group stand in a circle. Explain that one person will start the contest by giving his or her first variation ("If you run a red light, a police car will be sitting at the intersection"). The person to his or her right will go next, and so on around the circle. If a person cannot come up with a new variation in ten seconds, he or she is out. Continue until only one person remains in each group. If you have enough time, you might assemble the winners from each group and have them compete for the "grand championship."

Step 2
Have kids form teams of four. Ask each team to come up with a song passage that illustrates the feelings and/or principles of the Ecclesiastes verses. The teams may use existing songs or come up with their own (perhaps changing the lyrics to a current popular song). For instance, one team might use "Bohemian Rhapsody" by Queen ("Nothing really matters/Anyone can see/Nothing really matters/Nothing really matters to me"). Another might use "Dust in the Wind" by Kansas ("All we are is dust in the wind/Dust in the wind/Everything is dust in the wind"). After a few minutes, have each team perform its song, using any choreography or enhancements it thinks might make the presentation more entertaining. You will judge the acts as though they're in a talent show, and award prizes to the winning team.

OPTIONS

SESSION FOUR

Step 1
The Book of Ecclesiastes is perfect for jaded kids. It reflects the views of one who's tried practically everything and found it wanting. Instead of using Repro Resource 8, have teams improvise satirical skits in which an always sunny "positive thinker" tries to look on the bright side as he or she is (1) being robbed; (2) undergoing brain surgery without anesthesia; (3) being executed for a crime someone else committed; or (4) taking the driver's road test when nothing is going right. Then ask: **Do you just "keep smiling" when life seems rotten? Why or why not? What do you think is a more realistic attitude?** Point out that Ecclesiastes makes no effort to cover up the parts of life that seem meaningless and miserable.

Step 5
Kids may question whether life without God is meaningless, especially if they know happy non-Christians. Acknowledge that life without God may not feel pointless—and that the Christian life may not always feel great. Then play an audiotape of a non-English language being spoken. See whether kids can figure out what's being said. Ask: **Were these words meaningless?** (Only to someone who doesn't understand them.) **Could you get any meaning out of them if you didn't understand the language?** (Maybe a little, if there was visual content or a few familiar words.) **If you did understand the words, would you understand everything the speaker meant?** (Not necessarily.) Point out that in a similar way, the meaning of life is garbled when you aren't on speaking terms with God. Even if you do speak His "language," you don't necessarily understand everything that happens in this world. But life makes a lot more sense when you can communicate with its Creator.

Step 2
Kids who aren't familiar with biblical principles may be confused by the "everything is meaningless" discussion. After all, if work (especially homework) and achievements are meaningless, why bother doing anything? Help your kids see that Ecclesiastes refers to these things as meaningless *in the context of eternity*. To help make this point, try to find some news stories about people who were buried with their prized possesssions (a Cadillac, jewelry, etc.) when they died. If you can't find such stories, point out that the pharaohs of ancient Egypt were buried with vast riches, servants, and even pets. Briefly discuss the axiom, "You can't take it with you." Then ask: **Do you think there's any similarity between the statements "You can't take it with you" and "Everything is meaningless"? Explain.**

Step 4
Kids with little Bible background—and with considerable worldly background—may not be able to easily dismiss the philosophies represented by the vanity plates (on Repro Resource 9) as "meaningless." Give these kids a chance to voice their opinions. Ask for four volunteers to play the roles of the people who own the plates. Encourage each one to explain why he or she places such an emphasis on the activity represented by the plate—and why life might seem "meaningless" without that activity. After all of the volunteers have shared, use their specific comments as a reference as you go through the questions on Repro Resource 9.

Step 2
To brighten the mood of the group after going through the "meaningless" passages in Ecclesiastes, have your kids brainstorm a list of the *meaningful* things God has given us. Write group members' suggestions on the board as they're named. The list might include things like our relationship with Him, our relationship with other Christians, and our eternal future. After a few minutes, pause for a time of silent prayer so kids can thank God for the meaningful things in their lives.

Step 3
Ask: **Do you think our meeting together every week is "meaningless"? Why or why not?** It is hoped that most of your group members will agree that your meetings are *not* meaningless. If so, ask each person to name one thing about your meetings that are meaningful to him or her. Encourage *specific* answers, not responses like "I like the people here." The affirmation that comes from this activity should increase the level of fellowship among your kids.

76

OPTIONS

SESSION FOUR

MOSTLY GIRLS

MOSTLY GUYS

EXTRA FUN

Step 4
Some of the priorities expressed by the vanity plates may hit home with your group members. Give your girls an opportunity to share their feelings about these priorities—in a non-threatening way. Say: **Let's say one of these plates belongs to your best friend. How would you defend her if someone started making fun of her plates?** Encourage most of your group members to respond. If possible, try to cover all four plates.

Step 5
Rather than having your girls come up with their own vanity plates, call each of them sometime before the meeting and ask her to bring three things that describe or define her life. For instance, one of your girls might bring a musical instrument (or music book), a pair of basketball shoes, and a cross-stitch pattern to show that she spends a lot of time practicing music, playing sports, and making crafts. As you wrap up the session, have each of your girls present and explain the things she brought in. Then point out that having hobbies and working toward career and personal goals is not necessarily wrong—as long as we realize that they cannot compare in importance to the "meaningful," eternal things of God.

Step 1
Rather than going through Repro Resource 8, ask each of your guys to describe one of the worst days he ever had—a day in which everything seemed to go wrong. You might want to start the activity by describing one of *your* worst days. After everyone has shared, ask: **How many of you guys know what Murphy's Law is?** If no one knows, explain what it is. Then read some of the variations from Repro Resource 8—including "Everything is meaningless." Ask: **Do any of these statements sound like things you'd find in the Bible? They are.** Then move into Step 2.

Step 3
Ask your guys to name some of their favorite male athletes. Then ask: **What is it that motivates these guys and gives their professional lives meaning? Is it money? Fame? Their friends and family? A competitive nature? The desire to win? The desire to be the best?** Ask your guys which of these motivations they think are admirable and which aren't. Use this discussion to introduce the topic of the meaninglessness of "everything."

Step 1
At the end of Step 1, have kids form two teams. Announce that the teams will be competing in a "meaningless relay." Use cones or some other kind of markers to make a "track" around your meeting room. Explain that when you say, **Go,** the first member of each team will start jogging around the track. However, the two contestants will be running in *opposite* directions. After one lap, they'll tag the next person in line, who must skip around the track. The next person must hop; the person after that must gallop, the person after that must crawl backward; the person after that must do somersaults around the track; etc. Toward the end of the competition, just as kids are starting to get excited about winning, stop the race. Point out that it really doesn't matter who wins the race because, according to the Bible, everything is meaningless.

Step 5
Wrap up the session with a "nostalgia party." Play some music that was popular when your group members were in third or fourth grade. You might even want to have group members bring in their baby pictures and stage a "guess the identity" contest. During the party, ask your group members to look back on their (brief) lives so far and identify things that were meaningful and things that were meaningless. If you don't think your kids would be comfortable sharing these things aloud, have them write their responses anonymously on sheets of paper. After a few minutes, collect the sheets and read some of the responses aloud. Then lead in to the activity in the session in which the kids, pretending to be seventy years old, look back at what is meaningful and meaningless in their lives now.

OPTIONS

SESSION FOUR

Step 1
Instead of using Repro Resource 8, rent the video of the movie *City Slickers*. Play the scene early in the film in which a disillusioned Mitch Robbins (Billy Crystal) tells his son's classmates about the meaningless lives they can expect. The speech begins with "Value this time in your life, kids, because this is the time in your life when you still have your choices. . . ." It ends with "The eighties, you'll have a major stroke, and you end up babbling with some Jamaican nurse who your wife can't stand, but who you call Mama. Any questions?" Ask: **What questions would you want to ask if you were in that class? How do you feel about this view of life? Why do you think this character feels this way? Do you think people get more optimistic or more pessimistic as they grow older? Why?** Note that you're going to look at a remarkably similar picture of life—in the Bible, of all places.

Step 3
Sometime during this step, play a bleak, lamenting song like "The River" by Bruce Springsteen. Ask: **How is this song like the Book of Ecclesiastes? Does it offer any hope at all?** During Step 4, play a "searching" song like "River of Dreams" by Billy Joel. Ask: **What is this person searching for? What are the chances of finding it apart from God?** At the beginning of Step 5, play an upbeat but realistic contemporary Christian song like "Called to Hope" by Geoff Moore and the Distance. Ask: **What reasons for hope does this song give?**

Step 1
For a shorter opener, try the following activity. Have kids form pairs. Give each pair a pencil, a separate eraser, and a sheet of poster board. Each pair should put its poster board on the floor and kneel nearby. At your signal, one partner in each pair will write a passage from Ecclesiastes (you choose which one) on the poster board, while the other partner erases it as it's written. The first pair to write and erase its passage wins. Don't award a prize, though. Note the pointlessness of what kids just did—rushing and working, and then ending up with the same blank sheets they had in the beginning. Ask: Does life ever seem that way? Which parts of a typical day seem most pointless to you?

Step 2
Skip most of this step—except to read just one or two of the fifteen passages listed, explain the authorship of Ecclesiastes, and note the six often-repeated phrases and words mentioned at the end of the step. In Step 3, instead of having kids skim the fifteen passages for "meaningless" things, assign kids to look for them in some or all of the references listed in the second paragraph of Step 3. Of the "under the sun" passages listed in the fifth paragraph of the step, skip 1:3, 9, 14. Of the passages listed in the eighth paragraph, read only 2:24, 25.

Step 1
Urban variations of Murphy's Law probably should reflect more serious situations than paying full price for something. Use the following statements in your discussion of Repro Resource 8:
- **The Poverty Pit: Once you're down, you stay down.**
- **Godfather Pacino's Realization: Just when you think you're out, they pull you back in.**
- **The Ultimate End: You're better off dead.**
- **Urban Baseball Treatise: You can't win for losing.**

Step 3
Because many urban kids have done without "things" for most of their life, their goal may be to acquire as many possessions as possible when they get older. So calling material possessions "meaningless" may not make sense to them. You may want to approach the topic from another direction. Ask: **What are some of the wrong methods that people use to get money?** (Stealing from or robbing others, selling drugs or guns, selling their bodies in prostitution, etc.) **Would you be willing to use one or more of these methods to get money? Why or why not?** It's likely that at least some of your kids will say that having money is not worth the risks associated with the methods you named. Point out that similarly, having material possessions is not worth risking your relationship with God. Compared to the gifts God has in store for us, material possessions are worthless.

OPTIONS

SESSION FOUR

Step 1
Rather than distributing copies of Repro Resource 8, simply explain what Murphy's Law is and read a few variations from the sheet. Then distribute paper and pencils. Instruct your high schoolers to work together to come up with some more variations of Murphy's Law ("If you accept a part-time job, a better-paying one will become available the next day"). Instruct your junior highers, on the other hand, to work together to come up with *positive* variations of Murphy's Law ("If it's raining, there's something to do inside" or "If you paid full price for something, you'll get a bigger refund if you return it"). After about five minutes, see which group came up with the most variations.

Step 2
Explain that a certain key word and a certain key phrase are each used over thirty times in the Book of Ecclesiastes. Have your high schoolers and junior highers compete to see which group can figure out what word and phrase you're talking about—simply by scanning the Book of Ecclesiastes in their Bibles. Make sure all group members have the same translation, preferably the NIV. The first group to write the correct word ("meaningless") and phrase ("under the sun") on a piece of paper and bring it to you is the winner. You may want to award prizes to the winning group. Use the activity to lead in to your study of Ecclesiastes.

Step 2
As you go through the seemingly depressing sections in Ecclesiastes, challenge your group members to counter each downbeat passage with another Scripture passage that emphasizes the joy of serving the Lord and the happiness and fulfillment that come from living a Christian life. For instance, someone might counter Ecclesiastes 1:1-11 with Philippians 4:4-7.

Step 3
Have your group members compare some of the "meaningless" passages in Ecclesiastes (1:1, 14; 2:1, 11, 15, 17, 23; 4:7, 8; 5:10; 6:2, 9; 8:14; 11:8, 10) to Paul's comments in Philippians 3:2-11. Ask: **How are the things that Paul called "loss" and "rubbish" similar to the things the writer of Ecclesiastes called "meaningless"? How are they different?**

Date Used:

Approx. Time

Step 1: Is There a Flaw in Murphy's Law? _____
o Extra Action
o Large Group
o Heard It All Before
o Mostly Guys
o Extra Fun
o Media
o Short Meeting Time
o Urban
o Combined Jr. High/High School

Step 2: A Real Downer _____
o Extra Action
o Small Group
o Large Group
o Little Bible Background
o Fellowship & Worship
o Short Meeting Time
o Combined Jr. High/High School
o Extra Challenge

Step 3: A Meaningless Exercise _____
o Small Group
o Fellowship & Worship
o Mostly Guys
o Media
o Urban
o Extra Challenge

Step 4: Vanity Plates _____
o Little Bible Background
o Mostly Girls

Step 5: A Lot on Your Plate _____
o Heard It All Before
o Mostly Girls
o Extra Fun

79

SESSION 5
A Matter of Time

TIME TO BE BORN	TIME TO DIE	TIME TO PLANT	TIME TO UPROOT	TIME TO WEEP	TIME TO LAUGH	TIME TO MOURN	TIME TO DANCE

YOUR GOALS FOR THIS SESSION:
Choose one or more

☐ To help kids see that God is in control of all things.

☐ To help kids understand how different life is when they really believe that God is in control of everything that happens.

☐ To help kids affirm that God has set eternity in their hearts and wants them to share eternity with Him.

☐ Other _____

Your Bible Base:

Ecclesiastes 3:1-14

CUSTOM CURRICULUM

STEP 1

A Time to Get Started

(Needed: Copies of Repro Resource 10, pencils, dictionary [optional])

OPTIONS

To begin the session, pass out copies of "It's about Time" (Repro Resource 10) and pencils. This sheet lists in one column ten different time spans (from one second to one lifetime). In another column, ten different events are listed. Group members are to match the events with the appropriate time span. Kids may work in pairs or small groups to complete the sheet.

If you want to use the activity as a mixer, divide the group in half. Cut apart one or more copies (depending on the size of your group) of Repro Resource 10. Distribute the time span slips among one half of the group; distribute the events slips among the other half. Then give the kids a few minutes to pair up with the appropriate partner.

The correct answers are as follows:

• In one second/Eight million blood cells die within the average adult human
• In one minute/Forty-seven Bibles are distributed worldwide
• In one hour/A pig can run eight miles
• In one day/The average person laughs twenty times
• In one week/775 new books are published in the U.S.
• In one month/The average person cries one time
• In one year/The average person grows four new eyelashes
• In one decade/The average person's head sheds 247,520 hairs
• In one quarter-century/The average person takes 250 million breaths
• In one lifetime/The average person's heart beats 2.5 billion times

Afterward, ask: **Did any of these numbers surprise you? If so, which ones?** Let kids briefly share anything that they found interesting. It is pretty amazing to think that the human body generates millions of new blood cells every second. It's also interesting to note that people typically laugh 600 times more often than they cry.

Let's say some alien race got their hands—or tentacles, or whatever—on this sheet. If these aliens didn't know anything else about earthlings, what would they learn from this sheet? This is kind of a wild question that may or may not work for your group. If it works, have some fun with it. If it doesn't, hurry on to the next question and blame it on us. Some things the aliens might learn are that humans are complex creatures, that we read a lot, that we like to laugh,

81

and that we keep track of time in strange ways.

Today we're going to be looking at time and how we should view the passing of time in our lives. Each of us is given only so much of it. So, before we go any further, what exactly is time? You might want to bring in a dictionary and read the definitions listed there. One definition is "the measured or measurable period during which an action, process, or condition exists or continues: duration; a continuum which lacks spatial dimensions and in which events succeed one another from past through present to future."

Say: **Back in the 1970s, a guy named Jim Croce recorded a song called "Time in a Bottle." Ironically, he died in a plane crash shortly after recording it. If time *were* available in a bottle, how much do you think people would be willing to pay for it?** Get a few responses.

STEP 2

A Time to Think

(Needed: Bibles, paper, pencils, chalkboard and chalk or newsprint and marker)

Distribute paper (save a tree by using the back of Repro Resource 10) and pencils. Have group members write down their answers to the following nine questions:
1. What do you think you'll be doing ten seconds from now?
2. What do you think you'll be doing ten minutes from now?
3. What do you think you'll be doing ten hours from now?
4. What do you think you'll be doing ten days from now?
5. What do you think you'll be doing ten weeks from now?
6. What do you think you'll be doing ten months from now?
7. What do you think you'll be doing ten years from now?
8. What do you think you'll be doing ten decades from now?
9. What do you think you'll be doing ten centuries from now?

Afterward, have kids share some of their answers. Then ask: **Which answers are you least certain about? Which ones are you most certain about?** Kids will probably be least certain about what they'll be doing in ten years. Pay particular attention to how kids answered questions 8 and 9. Obviously, we'll all be dead and gone by then, but did any kids mention anything about their ultimate spiritual destiny? This is a concept you'll want to revisit later in the session.

82

Ask: **When it comes right down to it, how much control do you have over what happens in your life? Would you say you have total control, a lot of control, some control, very little control, or no control?** Let kids debate this for a while. There's no easy way to answer the question. In some ways, we have a lot of control over our actions and the choices we make. But on the other hand, we can't control a lot of things—nature, other people, time itself.

How does the passing of time make you feel? Chances are, many young people don't give it much thought. But they're probably aware that "older people" keep commenting on how quickly time goes by. With a question like this, you're starting to get closer to the crux of the issue. When we stop to think about it, we see that a lifetime comes and goes very quickly. If kids have trouble talking about this, ask them how they feel about getting older—much older. How do they think their parents feel about it? Why do some people dread getting older?

A Time to Study

(Needed: Bibles)

Say: **When we start thinking about time and the future, we can get pretty philosophical about it. That's exactly what happens to the writer of Ecclesiastes in the third chapter.**

Have kids turn to Ecclesiastes 3. Read aloud verses 1 through 14. If possible, stay together as one group to discuss the following questions. If your group is too large for that, feel free to photocopy these questions for any other discussion leaders.

The first eight verses talk about there being a time and a season for everything. Which of these things do people have the least control over? (Certainly a time to be born [vs. 2]. Most people also have no control over the time of their death [vs. 2]. Individuals may feel they have no control over times of war [vs. 8].)

Which ones would you question as to whether there's ever a proper time for? (Possibly a time to kill [vs. 3], a time to scatter or gather stones [vs. 5], a time to tear [vs. 7], a time to hate and a time for war [vs. 8].) Point out that there are two interpretations as to what it means to scatter or gather stones. Some people think it refers to building a house or tearing one down. Others see it as a reference to military action—scattering stones to ruin an enemy's field, or gathering stones to prepare the way for a leader, as seen in Isaiah 62:10. Let kids offer suggestions for when it might be appropriate to hate or kill. Instead of getting hung up on specific issues like capital punishment or euthanasia, help kids remember that the author is painting a vivid picture of our lives and pointing out to us that all things that happen are within God's control and happen according to His divinely appointed timetable. This becomes much clearer in verse 14.

Do you see any progression in the first eight verses, or any logical order to these pairings? (The passage starts with the most momentous events in our lives—birth and death [vs. 2], then covers other activities and events in our lives, including creating and destroying things [vss. 2, 3], human emotions [vs. 4], friends and enemies [vs. 5], material possessions [vss. 6, 7], and human relationships [vss. 7, 8]. It's hard to imagine an area of life that's not covered.)

How would you answer the question raised in verse 9? Why do you suppose the writer is raising this question now? (The simple truth is that all of our toil is for nothing if we have no lasting relationship with God. The writer is probably talking about more than one's job. Toil might be referring to all of the effort someone puts into life. When life is over, it might seem that it's all been for nothing. The writer raised the same point in Ecclesiastes 1:3. It's as if the writer is looking at the entire scope of one's lifetime and wondering what he's been working so hard for all of these years.)

Have someone read again Ecclesiastes 3:10, 11. Then ask: **What is the "burden" God has laid on people? How can something beautiful be burdensome?** If no one mentions it, point out that even though life can be beautiful, people will never be satisfied with created things because God has given us a hunger for eternal things. Even though we want to understand how it all fits together and what the future holds, we'll never fully understand God's ways here. To those who think about this hard enough, it can be a terrible burden—especially those who haven't found eternal life through Jesus.

What evidence is there that God has "set eternity" in people's hearts? (People of very diverse cultures throughout history have held some belief in a higher power and the hope of some type of eternal existence—that there's more to life than what we experience here on earth. Even with tremendous scientific advances, most people still cling to belief in a higher power. People also want to know what the future holds and understand how things work. People also have some sense of right and wrong—a moral conscience—that suggests that some truths are eternal. When God made us in His image [Genesis 1:27], He gave us a degree of likeness to Him. We are made for eternity, but our sin interrupted the unblemished relationship humans had. Nevertheless, we can live with God because of Christ.)

Who do you suppose would be least likely to agree with the writer's comments in verses 12 and 13 that there's noth-

ing better in life than to be happy, do good, eat and drink, and find satisfaction in our toil? (Probably people who aren't content with their lot in life. Some "religious" people might question whether there's more to life than this. The passage may seem kind of self-centered, especially if the "do good" part is translated "enjoy the good" as some Bible versions render it.) Point out that we have to keep in mind that the writer of Ecclesiastes didn't know all about God's plan and the grace He would extend through Jesus. [See II Timothy 1:10.]

Verse 14 is a great verse. What does it tell us about the things God does or allows to happen in our lives? (All of God's actions are permanent [they last forever]; they are complete [nothing can be added]; they are secure [nothing can be taken from them]; they are purposeful [so that we'll revere or worship Him].)

How does it make you feel to know that God is in total control of everything that happens? If no one mentions it, point out that the fact that God's control *should* make us feel secure and trusting. But in reality, we often lose sight of what it really means, and we end up fretting over things, especially the future.

A Time to Apply

(Needed: Bibles, chalkboard and chalk or newsprint and marker)

Ask your group members to call out terrible things that have happened in their lives or in the lives of other people—things like the death of a loved one, illness, loss of a job, natural disaster, etc. Write these things on the board as they are named.

Then ask: **What might someone who doesn't have faith in God say about a list like this?** (Perhaps that it proves He doesn't exist—otherwise, He wouldn't allow such terrible things to happen.)

What might someone who does have faith in God say about a list like this? (There's no way we'll ever understand why all of these things happen. But just because God allows them to happen doesn't mean He doesn't exist.)

Next, have group members list some of the biggest fears young people face as they look to the future—things like major decisions and responsibilities (like college, career, and marriage), being a victim of a violent crime, war, AIDS and other terminal diseases, etc. Write these things on the board as they are named.

Then ask: **What might someone who has no faith in God say about this list?** (Life is pretty frightening. How am I ever going to make it? What's the point, anyway?)

What might someone who does have faith in God say about a list like this? (Life is pretty frightening, but I know God is in control of all that happens to me. With that in mind, I can face the future, and I don't have to worry about what will happen.)

Finally, have group members list some of the things Christians hope for—things like heaven, eternal life, reuniting with loved ones, being with Jesus forever, etc. Write these things on the board as they are named.

Then say: **Some people might look at a list like this and call it "wishful thinking." Is it?** (Wishful, no; hopeful, yes. There is a difference. Christians believe in these things through faith in what God has promised. There are really only two logical conclusions a person can come to about the future—hope or despair. If God isn't in the picture, there's really no reason for hope.)

We've been talking a lot about eternity. What exactly is eternal life? You may need to point out that it's much more than the continuation of time forever. Look up John 17:3 together. Ask kids to comment on how this verse expands our view of eternal life. In it, we see that eternal life involves knowing Jesus. It's something we can begin experiencing here and now—and forever. Encourage any kids who haven't seriously considered a relationship with Jesus to talk with you more about it after the session.

A Time to Commit

(Needed: Bible, copies of Repro Resource 11, pencils)

Distribute copies of "The Bad and the Beautiful" (Repro Resource 11). This is an exercise in structured journaling, a written prayer activity that should help kids focus on the central message of Ecclesiastes 3. Have kids work individually to complete each sentence on the sheet. Then spend some time in prayer, allowing individuals to share what they've written. This would probably work best if you have several people share one section at a time. You could read aloud the words on the sheet and then pause for kids to read aloud what they've written. Be prepared to read some of your own responses too. To close the prayer time, read Psalm 93 or I Timothy 1:17.

S T R E E T W I S E

REPRO RESOURCE
10

IT'S ABOUT TIME

Match each event (in the right column) with the amount of time it takes for that event to happen (in the left column).

In one second   The average person cries one time

In one minute   The average person grows four new eyelashes

In one hour   A pig can run eight miles

In one day   The average person laughs twenty times

In one week   Forty-seven Bibles are distributed worldwide

In one month   775 new books are published in the U.S.

In one year   The average person's head sheds 247,520 hairs

In one decade   Eight million blood cells die within the average adult human

In one quarter-century   The average person takes 250 million breaths

In one lifetime   The average person's heart beats 2.5 billion times

STREETWISE

REPRO RESOURCE 11

The BAD AND *the Beautiful*

He has made everything beautiful in its time. He has also set eternity in the hearts of men; yet they cannot fathom what God has done from beginning to end. . . . I know that everything God does will endure forever; nothing can be added to it and nothing taken from it. God does it so that men will revere him (Ecclesiastes 3:11, 14).

Thank You, Lord, for the beautiful things in life like . . .

Thank You also for the certainty that You are still in control, even when really bad things happen like . . .

Help me to keep trusting in You even though I'm not sure about . . .

Augustine said, "You have made us for yourself, and our hearts are restless until they find peace in you."

Lord, thank You for setting eternity in my heart. Help me . . .

OPTIONS

SESSION FIVE

Extra Action

Step 1
You'll need one or more watches (the kind with hands) for this game. Each watch should have a knob on the side for setting the time. You'll also need stick-on labels, each big enough to cover a watch face. Have kids form groups. Instruct each group to stand in a circle. Cover the watch faces with labels; give each group a watch. Make sure the knob is pulled out so that the time can be reset. At your signal, members of each group will pass the watch back and forth across their circle. Each person who receives the watch must turn the dial forward or backward to randomly reset the time before passing it to someone else. When you call, **Time,** kids in each group will guess what time the watch says. Then pull off the labels to see whose guess was closest. Play as many rounds as you have time for (no pun intended). Then award a prize to the best guesser in each group. Use this activity to lead in to the last two questions in Step 1.

Step 3
Assign kids an action to go with each activity mentioned in Ecclesiastes 3:1-8 (hugging themselves for "embrace," hopping on one foot for "dance," etc.). Have group members stand in a wide-open space. Call out the "times" from the passage at random (**Time to plant! Time to search!**), pausing for just a few seconds after each one. Any person who doesn't recall and perform the correct action after an instruction is out. Do this, increasing the speed, until you're down to one or two winners. Afterward, ask: **Do you ever feel that there isn't enough time to do everything that needs doing? How does this relate to verses 9-14?**

Small Group

Step 1
At the end of the step, sit with your kids in a circle on the floor. Place an empty soft-drink bottle in the middle of the circle. Announce that you'll be playing "Spin the Bottle" (or, more specifically, a version of the game appropriate for a church youth group). After the bottle is spun, the person to whom it points must share one thing he or she would do if given an "extra bottle of time" (say, one year's worth). For instance, one group member might dedicate the entire year to becoming a guitar virtuoso. Another might use the extra time to see as many movies as possible. Another might take a year's worth of naps. Continue until all of your group members have shared at least once.

Step 2
In a small group, it's likely that your group members know each other fairly well. With this in mind, you might want to turn the prediction activity into a game. After kids have written their nine answers on a sheet of paper, collect the sheets. Then read aloud the responses one at a time and see if kids can guess who wrote what. The first person to correctly identify who wrote a particular response gets a point. The person with the most points at the end of the game is the winner. Use the questions in the session to discuss the activity.

Large Group

Step 1
Try a large-scale "Beat the Clock" contest as an opener for your large group. Have kids form teams. Give each team an assignment to complete some kind of stunt within one minute. Here are some stunts to consider:
• Team members, with their arms tied behind their back and their legs tied together, must get ten inflated balloons into a clothes basket.
• Team members, while wearing oven mitts, must arrange a deck of cards in a certain order.
• Team members, while blindfolded, must locate and stack a certain number of blocks.

If possible, try to have an adult volunteer (equipped with a stopwatch) observing each stunt. After a minute, have the teams rotate and try a new stunt. The team that successfully completes the most stunts within a minute is the winner. Use this activity to lead in to a discussion of how we should view the passing of time in our lives.

Step 4
Have kids form groups of four to six. Distribute several newspapers and news magazines to each group. Instruct each group to find articles that illustrate some terrible things that happen to people (loss of a loved one, natural disaster, etc.). Then have each group brainstorm what a person who has faith in God and a person who doesn't have faith might say about these terrible occurrences. Continue by having the groups list some of the biggest fears young people face as they look to the future. Then have each group answer the questions that follow in the session. After several minutes, have each group summarize its findings for everyone else.

OPTIONS

SESSION FIVE

HEARD IT ALL BEFORE

LITTLE BIBLE BACKGROUND

FELLOWSHIP & WORSHIP

Step 3
Looking at Ecclesiastes 3:1-8, kids may think, "So there's a time for everything. So what?" Help kids see that God has *preferred* times for these things, and that we need to think about the right and wrong times for them. Ask: **Which verse from the passage might encourage a radio "shock jock" to clean up his act?** (Verse 4—Some things shouldn't be laughed at.) **Which verses might be used to encourage recycling?** (Time to keep [vs. 6]; time to mend [vs. 7].) **Which verse summarizes the debate over how Christians should act toward AIDS victims?** (Time to embrace, time to refrain [vs. 5].) **How can we decide the right times for these things?** (By praying and considering what else the Bible says on these subjects.) Note that this passage's purpose is not to tell us when to do these things. Other Scripture passages help with that. For example, Matthew 25:31-46 could help Christians decide how to react to AIDS victims.

Step 4
For jaded kids and those who struggle with doubts, Steps 4 and 5 may sound like shallow, wishful thinking. If you think your kids will need more help with the question of God's control in a world filled with tragedy, you can either skip these steps—or be prepared for more in-depth discussion. You may want to plan an additional session, using a resource like *When Kids Ask Sticky Questions* (Cook). Instead of calling for commitment in Step 5, read Ecclesiastes 3:15-17, which implies that God will deal with this world's injustices. Instead of demanding that we ignore what's going on and be happy anyway, He promises to make things right—in His time. You may want to end with silent prayer, encouraging kids to express their feelings to God about this.

Step 3
Kids with little Bible background may wonder about the relevance of Ecclesiastes 3:1-14 in today's society. After all, probably very few of them have experienced a time to scatter or gather stones. So as a group, decide which of the events listed in the passage are easy to understand today and which aren't. Replace the ones that are hard to understand with other events kids face in their daily lives ("A time to study and a time to goof off," "A time to get some exercise and a time to rest," etc.). Then brainstorm some scenarios in which an event is done "out of time." For example, what if someone *laughed* when it was time to *weep* (perhaps at a funeral)? What if someone *tore down* when it was time to *build* (perhaps at a construction site)? If your group members enjoy performing, have them act out some of the scenarios. If not, just have them describe what the results might be.

Step 4
If your kids don't have much Bible background, they may have had their view of eternity colored by media portrayals of heaven, hell, and the afterlife. So it might be helpful to spend a few minutes going through the "basics" of what the Bible says about such topics. A helpful resource for this is *Unseen Mysteries* in the Custom Curriculum series. Focus specifically on Sessions 3 and 4, which deal with what the Bible says about heaven and hell. Don't spend too much time on this. Give kids just an overview of what eternity will be like.

Step 1
As your group members arrive, give each of them a slip of paper made out in the form of a blank check. It should have the current date on it; but other than that, all lines should be left blank. Explain: **This is a blank check. It's good for one thing—and that's whatever you want. If you could run out now and buy one thing you've always wanted, what would it be? Write the item on your check. On the line labeled "amount," write "Free." Then sign your name at the bottom.** Have kids pair up. Instruct them to share with their partners what they wrote and why. After a few minutes, say: **Now let's suppose you've all just found out that you're going to die in exactly one week. If you could, would you trade the item on your check for an extra year of life? How about an extra month? An extra week? An extra day?** Have your group members share their responses with their partners. Then, as a group, discuss why time is so important to us.

Step 5
As you wrap up the session, lead your group members in singing (or reviewing the lyrics of) a couple of hymns that deal with eternity or God's eternal nature. Among the hymns you might consider is "Amazing Grace" ("When we've been there ten thousand years . . ."). If your group members are reluctant to sing, play a recording of "The Hallelujah Chorus" ("He shall reign forever and ever . . ."). Afterward, have each group member try to describe eternity in a way a five year old could understand. However, he or she may not use the word *forever* in his or her description.

OPTIONS

SESSION FIVE

Mostly Girls

Step 2
In a group of mostly girls, you might want to consider using questions that are more specific than the ones listed in the session. For instance, you might ask: **How many of you think you'll be married ten years from now? Where do you think you and your husband will live ten years from now? How many kids do you think you'll have ten years from now? What do you think your career will be ten years from now?** Distribute paper and pencils. Instruct your group members to briefly sketch out their "ideal life" for the next ten years. After a few minutes, ask several volunteers to share what they wrote. Then introduce the topic of how much control we have over our lives.

Step 4
Have your group members refer to the "ideal life" sheets they created in Step 2 (see the option above). Ask: **What if some unexpected tragedies invaded your ideal life? For instance, what if one of your children died due to complications at birth? Or what if your marriage turned out to have some serious problems, and you and your husband separated? How would you deal with these issues? Would your faith in God make any difference in the way you responded?** Acknowledge that the future can be frightening. However, if we know that God is in control of all that happens, we don't *have* to worry about the future—even though sometimes we may forget that.

Mostly Guys

Step 2
Before the session, rent a radar gun (a device that tells you how fast something is moving) from your local batting cage or sporting goods store. You'll also need to bring in several mattresses (and any other "cushioning" material you can find) and three hard rubber balls (about the size of baseballs). Set up your room so that guys will be throwing at the mattresses. You (or another volunteer) will stand off to the side of the throwing lane, clocking the speed of your guys' pitches with the radar gun. Allow each guy three pitches, so he can gauge how fast he's throwing. Before his last pitch, he must predict the speed of the throw. If he's exactly right on his prediction, give him a prize. Afterward, ask your guys how much control they think they had over the speed of their pitches. Then ask them how much control they think they have in other areas of their life.

Step 5
Ask your guys to respond honestly to the following questions. Ask: **How hard is it for you to accept the fact that you're not in control of your own life? Explain. Do you ever wish that you could take control of your life away from God for a while so that you could do some things that you think are best? If so, what areas of your life would you most like to control?** Have someone read aloud Romans 8:28. Then ask: **Why is this sometimes hard to believe?**

Extra Fun

Step 1
Begin the session with a variation of the game "Telephone." Have your kids form two teams. Instruct the members of each team to sit in a line, facing forward. Give the person at the back of each line a sheet of paper and a pencil. Instruct him or her to draw something—perhaps an elephant (but do it quietly so that no one else can hear what you say). Give the person ten seconds to draw; then have him or her pass the paper and pencil to the person in front of him or her. The next person will then continue the first person's drawing, not knowing what the picture is supposed to be. Continue until everyone has had a chance to draw. Then have each team hold up its finished picture while you announce what it was *supposed* to be. Afterward, ask: **What would have been a quicker and more time-efficient way to get this picture drawn?** (Have one person draw it according to instructions.) **What are some ways people waste time in their everyday lives?** Get responses from several group members.

Step 5
As you wrap up the session, prepare a time capsule. Ask your group members to bring in items that represent the current era (e.g., a T-shirt with the logo of a popular brand of athletic apparel on it, a videotape of TV shows that are currently popular, audiotapes of music that is currently popular, etc.)—things that are likely to become "dated" in a few years. Also have kids write out Bible verses that speak of the promises of God—which *don't* change over time (particularly those that deal with His promise to us of eternal life). Place these verses in the time capsule as well. If possible, try to "bury" the time capsule somewhere in your church—perhaps in that messy storage closet. Put a note in there to the youth group of twenty years from now.

OPTIONS

S E S S I O N   F I V E

Step 1
Show a time-travel scene from one or more of the following videos: *Time after Time, Time Bandits, Bill and Ted's Excellent Adventure, Star Trek IV, The Philadelphia Experiment,* one of the *Back to the Future* films, etc. Be sure to screen the scenes for appropriateness first. Then ask: **What kinds of things usually happen in time-travel movies? How about in movies that show a character being frozen and then thawed out in the future—like *Demolition Man, Sleeper,* and *Forever Young*? What appeals to you about being able to free yourself from the grip of time? What doesn't?**

Step 4
Rent the video of *Dead Poets Society*. Show the trophy case scene (after first screening it yourself) about ten minutes into the film, in which John Keating (Robin Williams) teaches his *"Carpe diem"* ("Seize the day") philosophy. Ask: **How is this philosophy like the philosophy in Ecclesiastes 9:7? How is it different? How could it lead to a meaningful life? How could it lead to selfishness or ignoring God?**

Step 1
Skip Step 1. For Step 2, bring a VCR remote control. Announce that this high-tech device can alter time, fast-forwarding whole youth groups into the future. Have the group "travel" into the future by the increments mentioned in the session's nine questions. For example, point the remote, push "Fast Forward," and say: **We have now traveled ten seconds into the future. What are you doing?** Kids should pantomime what they expect to be doing then, and at each of the other eight intervals as you announce them. Have volunteers explain their actions. Then discuss as instructed in the session.

Step 3
Instead of using the first three questions in Step 3, condense the discussion of Ecclesiastes 3:1-14 by asking this: **Do you think these things happen at the "right" times in most people's lives? Why or why not? How could we do a better job of doing things at the right times?** Then move into the session's discussion of verses 9-14. To save more time, skip the last question in Step 3 and go directly to the last question in Step 4. In Step 5, instead of instructing kids to fill out Repro Resource 11, work your way around the circle (or up and down rows) as each person chooses one of the first three incomplete sentences on the sheet and completes it out loud.

Step 2
Give each group member a paper plate and a marker. On the plate, kids should create a "life clock." Explain that for this exercise, you will assume that group members will live 72 years. So group members should write multiples of 6 on the clock face in place of the numbers (1-12) that normally go there. In place of "1," kids should write "6" (representing 6 years of age); in place of "2," they should write "12" (representing 12 years of age); in place of "3," they should write "18" (representing 18 years of age); and so on, until they reach 72. Have kids mark the spot on the clock that represents their age now; then have them shade in the area back to 12 o'clock, representing the years they've already lived. On the rest of the clock, have kids write near the appropriate numbers the things they foresee themselves doing at that age. (For instance, they might write "Graduate from college" near 21.) After a few minutes, have volunteers display and explain their clocks.

Step 4
If you think your kids might be reluctant to share some of the terrible things that have happened to them, their families, or people they know, try another approach. Show scenes (which you've screened beforehand) from movies like *Boyz N the Hood, New Jack City, Menace II Society,* etc. that show the effects of urban violence. Then ask: **What might someone who doesn't have faith in God say about tragedies like these? What might someone who *does* have faith in God say about them?**

OPTIONS

SESSION FIVE

Step 2
As a group, brainstorm a list of things that have been created for the purpose of saving time. Your list might include microwave ovens, dishwashers, remote controls, computers, fax machines, fast-food restaurants, etc. After you've listed the items on the board, stage a mini-debate. Have your junior highers argue that the things on the list have made our lives better because they've freed up time for us to spend on other activities. Have your high schoolers argue that the things on the list have made our lives worse because they've caused us to become lazy and impatient. After the debate, discuss how much control we actually have over time and the things in our lives.

Step 4
Have kids prepare for a game of musical chairs. As much as possible, try to have junior highers standing next to high schoolers for the game. Explain that this version of musical chairs will not include music. Instead, kids will walk around the circle until a designated junior higher yells, "Stop!" At that point, a mad scramble for the chairs will ensue. The person who does not get a seat is out, and the game continues. [NOTE: Your junior highers could all gain an advantage if they planned a strategy with the designated person for when he or she will yell "Stop!" For instance, the person might give a signal (e.g., a cough) just before he or she yells.] Your high schoolers may complain that the junior highers have an unfair advantage because they're in control of what happens. Regardless, let the game continue until you have a winner (who *should* be the designated junior higher). Afterward, say: **This game may not have been very fair, but it can serve as a reminder to us that we have very little control over our lives—especially the timetable of our future.**

Step 2
Distribute paper and pencils. Instruct your group members to write down everything they can remember that they did yesterday. They should be as specific as possible as they list items. Explain that in addition to the "major" events, you're looking for things as minute and insignificant as "I waved at Mark on my way to English class" or "I asked my mom what's for dinner." After a few minutes, collect the papers. Explain to your kids that you'll refer to the sheets later in the session. Later, at the end of Step 4, read some of the lists aloud. As a group, determine which of the items on the lists might have "eternal significance." Certainly things like reading the Bible (or going to youth group meetings) might have eternal significance. But what about things like hanging out with friends, watching TV, or playing video games? Afterward, ask: **How much of our time should be spent doing things that have eternal significance? Explain.**

Step 3
One of the most intriguing parts of the Ecclesiastes 3 passage is the phrase "He [God] has . . . set eternity in the hearts of men." Explore this concept further with your group. Ask: **How has God set eternity in our hearts? If God has set eternity in our hearts, why do we need the Bible? Why can't some people recognize what God has set in their heart? What "proof" is there that we have eternity in our hearts?**

Date Used:

Approx. Time

Step 1: A Time to Get Started _____
o Extra Action
o Small Group
o Large Group
o Fellowship & Worship
o Extra Fun
o Media
o Short Meeting Time

Step 2: A Time to Think _____
o Small Group
o Mostly Girls
o Mostly Guys
o Urban
o Combined Jr. High/High School
o Extra Challenge

Step 3: A Time to Study _____
o Extra Action
o Heard It All Before
o Little Bible Background
o Short Meeting Time
o Extra Challenge

Step 4: A Time to Apply _____
o Large Group
o Heard It All Before
o Little Bible Background
o Mostly Girls
o Media
o Urban
o Combined Jr. High/High School

Step 5: A Time to Commit _____
o Fellowship & Worship
o Mostly Guys
o Extra Fun

Custom Curriculum Critique

Please take a moment to fill out this evaluation form, rip it out, fold it, tape it, and send it back to us. This will help us continue to customize products for you. Thanks!

1. Overall, please give this *Custom Curriculum* course (*Streetwise*) a grade in terms of how well it worked for you. (A=excellent; B=above average; C=average; D=below average; F=failure) Circle one.

    A   B   C   D   F

2. Now assign a grade to each part of this curriculum that you used.

a. Upfront article	A	B	C	D	F	Didn't use
b. Publicity/Clip art	A	B	C	D	F	Didn't use
c. Repro Resource Sheets	A	B	C	D	F	Didn't use
d. Session 1	A	B	C	D	F	Didn't use
e. Session 2	A	B	C	D	F	Didn't use
f. Session 3	A	B	C	D	F	Didn't use
g. Session 4	A	B	C	D	F	Didn't use
h. Session 5	A	B	C	D	F	Didn't use

3. How helpful were the options?
    - ❏ Very helpful
    - ❏ Somewhat helpful
    - ❏ Not too helpful
    - ❏ Not at all helpful

4. Rate the amount of options:
    - ❏ Too many
    - ❏ About the right amount
    - ❏ Too few

5. Tell us how often you used each type of option (4=Always; 3=Sometimes; 2=Seldom; 1=Never)

	4	3	2	1
Extra Action	❏	❏	❏	❏
Combined Jr. High/High School	❏	❏	❏	❏
Urban	❏	❏	❏	❏
Small Group	❏	❏	❏	❏
Large Group	❏	❏	❏	❏
Extra Fun	❏	❏	❏	❏
Heard It All Before	❏	❏	❏	❏
Little Bible Background	❏	❏	❏	❏
Short Meeting Time	❏	❏	❏	❏
Fellowship and Worship	❏	❏	❏	❏
Mostly Guys	❏	❏	❏	❏
Mostly Girls	❏	❏	❏	❏
Media	❏	❏	❏	❏
Extra Challenge (High School only)	❏	❏	❏	❏
Sixth Grade (Jr. High only)	❏	❏	❏	❏

BUSINESS REPLY MAIL
FIRST CLASS MAIL   PERMIT NO 1   ELGIN IL

POSTAGE WILL BE PAID BY ADDRESSEE

Attn: Youth Department
David C Cook Publishing Co
850 N GROVE AVE
ELGIN IL 60120-9980

(tape here)

NO POSTAGE NECESSARY IF MAILED IN THE UNITED STATES

---

6. What did you like best about this course?

7. What suggestions do you have for improving *Custom Curriculum*?

8. Other topics you'd like to see covered in this series:

9. Are you?
   ❑ Full time paid youthworker
   ❑ Part time paid youthworker
   ❑ Volunteer youthworker

10. When did you use *Custom Curriculum*?
    ❑ Sunday School   ❑ Small Group
    ❑ Youth Group   ❑ Retreat
    ❑ Other _____

11. What grades did you use it with? _____

12. How many kids used the curriculum in an average week? _____

13. What's the approximate attendance of your entire Sunday school program (Nursery through Adult)? _____

14. If you would like information on other *Custom Curriculum* courses, or other youth products from David C. Cook, please fill out the following:

   Name: _____
   Church Name: _____
   Address: _____
                _____
   Phone: (____) _____

                          Thank you!